Becoming Diddy:

The Making of Sean John Combs

From Mogul to Monster

By Darryl James

Becoming Diddy

"The music business is a cruel and shallow money trench, a long plastic hallway where thieves and pimps run free and good men die like dogs. There's also a negative side." —Hunter S. Thompson

Becoming Diddy: The Making of Sean John Combs, From Mogul to Monster, Copyright 2024 by Darryl James. All rights reserved. Printed in the United States of America. No part of this book may be used or reproduced in any manner whatsoever without written permission except in the case of brief quotations embodied in critical articles and reviews. For information, contact the publisher, Tenacious Books at (800) 481-0016.

FIRST EDITION

James, Darryl

Becoming Diddy: The Making of Sean John Combs, From Mogul to Monster, 1st ed.

ISBN: 9798218555986

Tenacious Books, Publisher

8939 S. Sepulveda Bl. #102

Los Angeles, CA 90045

Acknowledgements

Special thanks to Preston James for helping to discuss the concept of this book and crystallize it before I launched the project. Thanks to Greg "Greedy Greg" Jesse, Juliana Bolden, Billy Johnson, Jr., Peter Watts, Dr. April M. Clay, Ronda Dixon, Alonzo "Lonzo" Williams, Michael Charles Marsh, Dr. Letitia Bradley, my two Confidential Sources and to Sean John "Diddy" Combs for being the monster he is and always has been.

Becoming Diddy

The Making of Sean John Combs

(From Mogul to Monster)

By Darryl James

Introduction

Context.

As of the writing of this book, Sean John "Diddy" Combs is in prison awaiting trial for sex trafficking, racketeering conspiracy and transportation to engage in prostitution. He has been denied bail more than once, to be held in custody until the trial, which is set to begin in the Spring of 2025.

Many of the people who are writing about Sean John Combs are dealing with things that are, frankly, very recent.

They are also writing without context. The topic of Diddy is so hot that media outlets are clamoring for the latest tidbit of information that some information fails the smell test.

If the writing community is to do a service to the readers, we must provide some context to the information that is floating around.

Providing context means to take the newest hot pieces of information and help the reader to understand them, and to place them in perspective.

That's what I've set out to do with this book ***Becoming Diddy: The Making of Sean John Combs, From Mogul to Monster.***

I've collected some of the information that has been floating around, so that I can place it in perspective.

I also garnered information from two confidential sources who worked directly with Diddy. I interviewed a psychologist to understand how Diddy, the sexual predator/abuser's mind works; an attorney to summarize and give understanding to the charges Diddy faces; a theologian to understand how Combs operated as a sexual abuser while promoting God as a part of his lifestyle; and some of the people who viewed him closely over the years to understand his transition from mogul to monster.

And, I have my own perspective of Diddy.

By the time Sean "Puffy" Combs entered the music industry, I was already a veteran journalist and the Publisher/Editor of the second largest rap music publication, *Rap Sheet*. I had been the Executive Editor of *Rap Pages* (under the name Willie Wise), and I had written for *The Source*. I was also the Editor and Producer of the *Hip Hop Countdown & Report*, the only nationally syndicated Hip Hop radio show.

Under *Rap Sheet*, we produced the first Rap Music Convention, *Working Towards a Unified Hip Hop*

Nation, in Los Angeles, Atlanta and Washington, DC.

In 1994, I testified in the Senate at the Senate Hearings Against Hip Hop.

We produced the first Hip Hop Pay-Per-View Concert in 1995, *Free Expression in The Nineties*.

I watched Bad Boy develop when Puffy left Arista (under Uptown Records with Andre Harrell) and started Bad Boy Records. The marketing for the launch was nothing short of genius. The first artist was Craig Mack, and when they were preparing the Notorious B.I.G., the message was "B.I.G. Mack." Genius.

In short time, a rift between Tupac Shakur and B.I.G., turned into an all-out war between Death Row Records and Bad Boy Records.

Contrary to bad reporting by mainstream media, and cult-like ignorance of industry minions and the general public, there was NEVER a war between east coast rappers and west coast rappers. Silly people tried to make it larger than it was, but it was just between the two labels.

If I had taken sides in the war between those labels, I would have chosen Death Row. I grew in Hip Hop with N.W.A., because I had moved to Los Angeles, and because their music meant a great deal to me, aside from being dope. Also, I had come to respect the legendary music production of Andre Young, aka Dr. Dre.

But I never took sides in the wars between the splintered members of N.W.A. I rocked with Ice Cube when he made *Amerikkka's Most Wanted*, and

I became friends with Eric Wright, aka Eazy-E, before his untimely death.

I was in the studio with Dr. Dre when he was making *The Chronic* and I got to spend time with a young Calvin Broadus, aka Snoop Doggy Dogg, while he was making *Doggystyle*.

And, I never had any issues with Marion "Suge" Knight.

Rap Sheet covered Craig Mack and of course, B.I.G.

Just as we covered Dre, Snoop and Tupac.

But we stayed out of the fracas that ensued when both camps lost their shining stars, Tupac and Biggie Smalls.

Because that's when all the hell broke loose.

And it was around that time when the music industry insiders began to hear about the early unravelling of Sean John Combs.

But how did Diddy end up at the bottom of his life?

How did he go from a celebrated entertainment mogul to a legally embattled monster, accused of sex crimes involving underaged girls and boys as well as adult men and women?

These are the questions I will examine in this book, ***Becoming Diddy, the Making of Sean John Combs, From Mogul to Monster.***

This is the story of Puff Daddy, Puffy, P-Diddy, aka Diddy, the man, the music mogul, the monster.

Darryl James, Author

Becoming Diddy

Chapter One—Trapping the Monster

On Monday, September 16, 2024, federal authorities in New York arrested Sean John "Diddy" Combs for sex trafficking, racketeering conspiracy and transportation to engage in prostitution. At his arraignment, U.S. Magistrate Robyn Tarnofsky ordered him held without bail.

One of his attorneys, Marc Agnifilo, appealed the decision to hold him without bail, but lost with prosecutors arguing that Combs "poses an ongoing and significant danger to the community, has repeatedly engaged in obstructive conduct, and presents a serious risk of flight."

Agnifilo insisted that Combs was innocent and that he would fight the charges until he was cleared and free.

"He's been looking forward to this day," Agnifilo said. "He's been looking forward to clearing his name, and he's going to clear his name."

The arrest was apparently no surprise to Puffy, who was living in anticipation of an arrest and a trial. He was aware that Homeland Security had been investigating him. The key to his awareness was when Homeland Security raided his properties in LA and Miami.

In May of 2024, the U.S. Justice Department made CNN aware that they planned to indict Combs. They also said that they had been interviewing Combs' accusers and preparing them to testify in front of a federal grand jury.

As I write this, Sean John "Diddy" Combs remains in prison, having had bail denied more than once. According to U.S. Attorney Damian Williams: "As alleged in the Indictment, for years, Sean Combs used the business empire he controlled to sexually abuse and exploit women, as well as to commit other acts of violence and obstruction of justice. Today, he is charged with racketeering and sex trafficking offenses. If you have been a victim of Combs' alleged abuse – or if you know anything about his alleged crimes – we urge you to come forward. This investigation is far from over."

In October of 2024, Tony Buzbee, an attorney based in Houston, held a news conference calling for victims of Sean John Combs, expressing that he would represent them in a pursuit to receive financial compensation at the hands of the disgraced music mogul.

Buzbee claimed to have garnered more than three thousand calls in response to that public call. He told the BBC that he has confirmed numerous potential civil cases against Combs that are "probably in the 300 range," adding to the twenty lawsuits he has filed on behalf of men and women who have been abused. He estimates the final total to be between 100 and 150, after sorting out the cases that are subject to an expiration of the statute of limitations.

Buzbee, a former marine and television show host, started his legal profession representing complainants against a BP oil refinery that exploded and killed fifteen people.

The indictment against Diddy alleges that between at least "2008 and the present, Combs abused, threatened and coerced women and others, and led a racketeering conspiracy that engaged in sex trafficking, forced labor, kidnapping, arson, bribery, and obstruction of justice, among other crimes victims to fulfill his sexual desires, protect his reputation and conceal his conduct."

Also, according to the indictment, Combs "manipulated women to participate in highly orchestrated performances of sexual activity with male commercial sex workers." Combs also allegedly arranged for women and commercial sex workers to be flown to him.

Combs "ensured participation from the women by, among other things, obtaining and distributing narcotics to them, controlling their careers, leveraging his financial support and threatening to cut off the same, and using intimidation and violence," the indictment alleges.

Diddy, knowing that arrest was imminent, started to become unhinged.

According to one of his former Bad Boys Records artists, Mason Betha, professionally known as Ma$e, the timing of the raids by Homeland Security at Diddy's Miami and Los Angeles homes on Monday (March 25, 2024), was eerie and nothing short of amazing.

"It's amazing that all of this would transpire on that day," said Ma$e, to his *It Is What It Is* podcast co-host, Cam'Ron, referring to the federal raids occurring on the 27th anniversary of Christopher Wallace pka Notorious B.I.G.'s *Life After Death* album.

Voletta Wallace, B.I.G.'s mother told Rolling Stone Magazine that Diddy's legal issues make her sick to her stomach.

"I'm praying for Cassie," she said. "I'm praying for his mother. I don't want to believe the things that I've heard, but I've seen [the hotel video from 2016 of Diddy viciously attacking Cassie Ventura]. I pray that he apologizes to her.

"I hope that I see Sean one day, and the only thing I want to do is slap the daylights out of him. And you can quote me on that because I liked him. I didn't want to believe all the awful things, but I'm so ashamed and embarrassed."

The raids placed the 54-year-old Combs in the middle of a Homeland Security sex trafficking investigation, that currently has hundreds of alleged victims prepared to testify against him.

In a public statement, Combs' attorney Aaron Dyer, emphasized his client's presumed innocence.

"There has been no finding of criminal or civil liability with any of these allegations," he said. "Mr. Combs is innocent and will continue to fight every single day to clear his name... [This] unprecedented ambush led to a premature rush to judgment of Mr. Combs and is nothing more than a witch hunt based on meritless accusations made in civil lawsuits."

Yet, according to Attorney Buzbee, the number of potential civil lawsuits are "probably in the 300 range."

In addition to the trafficking charges, Combs faces charges of sexual assault, rape, and other heinous crimes levelled by a number of women, including Casandra "Cassie" Ventura, his ex-girlfriend, whom he was caught on videotape beating and kicking at a hotel.

Out of all the confirmed charges and pending charges, Attorney Ronda R. Dixon, Esq., said that she is most concerned about The Mann Act being used against Combs.

Ms. Dixon earned her Juris Doctorate at the University of California at Davis and has enjoyed a long and distinguished career in the music industry and in criminal law.

The Mann Act, previously called the White Slave Act of 1910, was connected to Jack Johnson, a famous boxer.

Dixon explains that "It was written specifically for him (Johnson), and they are applying it to Diddy's case. In Johnson's case, he was married to a white woman and in Georgia it was against the law for a Black man to be married to a white woman.

"We as Black people should actually be up in arms about some of this. Some of these cases were consensual. One of the women said that she didn't know that she was a victim until the FBI came and showed her a picture. The feds don't usually get involve in sex crimes. Also, usually, sex crimes have to involve people who are underage and there has to be force.

Dixon said that she's not defending Diddy, she just has an issue with the feds using the Mann Act to make a federal case against him, when the charges should be prosecuted at the state level.

"They are using The Mann Act to make his case federal. The Act was used to criminalize many kinds of relationships. In Jack Johnson's case, he was married to a white woman."

Dixon believes that the feds jumping into the mix "had to be based on some kind of sensationalism."

"I don't think the Mann Act should have come into play. I don't know how things became federal.

"Cassie's beating happened in the Century Plaza Hotel in Los Angeles, and they claim that's what initiated the legal action. But they came to LA from New York, not DC."

"It's not against the law to have sex, or to have orgies, if people are participating with consent."

And, Combs is also facing charges under the Racketeering Influenced and Corrupt Organizations Act (RICO).

"They are claiming that his business was a criminal enterprise. And his assistant was picked up to make it a conspiracy. Conspiracy is when one or more people agree to enter into a criminal enterprise. They're saying his employees were hired prostitutes—male and female.

"They might have jumped the gun picking him up if the statute of limitations on any of the charges have run out. Most felonies have three-year limitations. But that doesn't include certain classes, like sex crimes, with minors."

Since the charges are federal, Dixon believes that there is one trump card that can be played to Diddy's benefit.

"He could still get pardoned by you know who."

Dixon's theory is based on the popular view that President Donald Trump is on Diddy's infamous sex tapes, and that he could therefore pardon Diddy to halt the legal proceedings and prevent any tape of the president from going public.

However, even with a federal pardon, Combs would not be completely out of hot water.

"He could still face state charges in a number of states, including Florida, New York, or California. He was doing his Freak Offs in LA and other cities. Those states could still pursue him."

Chapter Two: Becoming The Mogul

Sean John Combs was born in Harlem, New York, on November 4, 1969, to parents Melvin Earl Combs and Janice Combs.

The year 1969 was pivotal for music and Harlem for the future entertainment mogul. That year, the city hosted the Harlem Cultural Festival from June 29 to August 24. Dubbed the Black Woodstock, the event attracted over 300,000 people to Mount Morris Park (now Marcus Garvey Park) and featured performances from icons Mahalia Jackson, Stevie Wonder, Gladys Knight and the Pips, Nina Simone, and more.

Born just a few months later, Sean is the eldest of the then-burgeoning young couple's two children.

Melvin, a late U.S. Air Force veteran, and taxi driver, was mentioned in *The New York Times* for being a drug dealer with an association with Frank Lucas, the Harlem drug kingpin who would be the subject of the 2007 Denzel Washington film "American Gangster." Janice was a former model. Both were known for their keen fashion sense, as displayed in old photos. Janice and Melvin deserve some credit for influencing their fashion designer son's love for clothes. "I'm a fashionable-type person. My husband was a fantastic dresser. It seems to have worn off," Janice told *The New Yorker*.

In an alleged drug-related incident, Melvin was fatally shot in his car in 1972 in Central Park West at 33 years old. Sean doesn't have many memories of his father. In the 2006 documentary *Portrait in*

Black and White, Sean vividly reflects on his father playing with him and throwing him in the air. "I remember the feeling I had," he said. "So anytime I would go on a roller coaster, I would think about my father. That same feeling I had in my stomach." Sean did not know the truth about how his father died until he began his studies at Howard University in Washington D.C. in 1987. His mother told him that his father died in a car accident, but that story never felt right, Sean said during his Howard University commencement speech in 2014 when he received an honorary doctorate degree. "Something in my soul was telling me otherwise," he said. "So, as soon as I got here, I went to the library and did some research. I used the microfilm at Founders (library) and searched through all the newspapers. And when I typed in my father's name, and the day he died, I read in the Amsterdam News that he had been murdered in a drug deal gone bad. Right there in that library, I realized there is nothing greater than a mother's love and her desire to protect her child. Nothing. I also decided that I would live my life in a way to make her proud. I decided to embrace the entrepreneurial spirit of my father but in an honest way. God bless you, Melvin Combs. I can feel you right next to me. But in an honest way, a legal way. By earning, scraping, working harder, believing in myself, and most importantly, making the most of the blessings that God blessed me with."

After Melvin's death, Janice worked three jobs to provide for Sean and his younger sister Keisha. She drove a school bus, taught at a daycare, and cared for children with cerebral palsy.

While Janice raised Sean and Keisha as Catholic and Sean was an altar boy, she also taught him to be tough. In the *Portrait in Black and White* documentary, Sean recalled the time his grandmother, who helped raise him and his sister, sent him to the store to buy some cigarettes, and he was beaten up and robbed by another kid. When he returned crying without the money or cigarettes, his mother demanded that he get the money back. "My mother was raising me for the real world," he said. "She always taught me that if someone hit me make sure I hit them back harder. Make sure they never hit me again."

The family left Harlem for the suburb Mount Vernon in 1981 when Sean was 11. This is where Sean's entrepreneurial spirit kicked in. His first job was as a paperboy, Janice told *The New Yorker*. "He came home one day and told me he wanted to start a paper route," she said. "That is how he started. He always wanted to work and make his money. We had a Cadillac car and a house, and he liked life like that." According to *Sean Combs Hip-Hop Biographies*, he spent one summer with an Amish family in Pennsylvania when attending a Fresh Air Fund camp.

Sean also became sexually active at a young age. "I had sex for the first time when I was 12," he revealed in *Portrait in Black and White*. He watched pornographic movies on Midnight Blue, a sexually themed public access program that aired on Manhattan Cable Television Channel J in New York from 1974 to 2003. "The first time I had sex, I wasn't scared. It felt so good to me," he explains with a mischievous grin. "I was really impressed by the way I was stroking this young lady. I remember she had like the best pussy in the world, even today. But I just remember how impressed I was. I used to watch Midnight Blue, and how I felt I was just as good as the porno stars I saw in Midnight Blue."

Sean played football for his high school Mount Saint Michael Academy in the Bronx, helping them win a division title in 1986. In an interview with *Gang Land News*, Head Coach Mario Valentini described Sean as a "good defensive back" and added that Sean earned his "Puff" nickname by "puffing out his chest to make himself look bigger and stronger than he was." Diddy received the nickname when he was younger because of his attitude. "Whenever I got mad as a kid, I used to always huff and puff," Sean told *Jet* magazine in

1998. "I had a temper. That's why my friend started calling me Puffy."

As the first person in his family to attend college, Sean was excited to enroll in Howard University in 1987 as a freshman business major. During his commencement speech, he reflected on his first impression of the prestigious HBCU. "My mind was blown," he said. "See, I'm from New York. New York is its own world, and I rarely traveled outside of New York. My mind was blown when I saw so many beautiful shades of brown. I never heard so many accents. Never seen so many beautiful women."

Enamored by the campus social life, Sean spent much time hanging out in the quad. He began throwing parties, even inviting rapper Slick Rick to an event. He also worked as a background dancer and appeared in music videos for Stacy Lattisaw, Big Daddy Kane, Father MC, and Heavy D, who was also from Mount Vernon.

Set on following in the footsteps of Def Jam Founder Russell Simmons, Sean asked Heavy D to refer him for an internship at his label Uptown Records. After pleading with label president Andre Harrell to give him a chance, Sean was hired. Sean caught the train from Washington, D.C. to New York every week for free and was soon promoted to work in the A&R department. "I just loved the music," Sean said in *Portrait in Black and White*. "Just like a drug to me. ... I started throwing parties. Being an entrepreneur. A hustler. The next Russell Simmons. I was working in the A&R department. They was paying me like $10,000 a year. A dress shirt and a tie. Yes sir. And the breakfast, the coffee, to getting the tapes. I remember I wanted to get everything quicker than everybody else got it. I went from there to getting a chance to being an A&R director to being the person everybody asked if it was hot or not because I'd be in the clubs all night."

After completing two years at Howard, Sean dropped out of school to work full-time. He moved into Harrell's house. Sean became Vice President at 20 years old and launched the careers of superstars Jodeci and Mary J. Blige, who went platinum.

Moving up the ranks fast, Sean could not be stopped. "I went to MCA Records in LA, and I was just cursing everybody out because they were like older white men, and they were trying to tell us how to make R&B music. We can't let nobody fuck it up. We just got to make sure that we stay true to who we are. ... I felt like I was Russell Simmons. I felt like my dream has come true."

Chapter Three: Hollywood Grooming

Sexual grooming accusations are a common theme in the more than one hundred sexual assault claims against Sean Diddy Combs.

According to WebMD, sexual grooming is described as "when a sexual predator builds a relationship with a child or adult to abuse and exploit them. They build trust but use it to control, isolate, and abuse their victims emotionally, physically, and sexually."

Given that the predator's ability to isolate his victims is one of the key components of sexual grooming, parents and guardians must consider what measures they need to employ to safeguard their children.

Sexual grooming of child stars has been ingrained in the entertainment industry since the emergence of Hollywood cinema in the early twentieth century.

Late child star Shirley Temple said Metro-Goldwyn-Mayer producer Arthur Freed exposed himself to her during their first meeting in his office when she was 11 years old in 1941.

In her autobiography, "Child Star," released nearly 50 years later in 1988, Temple said she met with Freed alone; her mother did not sit in on her one-on-one with her new boss. After Freed informed Temple that he wanted her to lose weight, get a new hairstyle, and take singing and tap dance lessons, he added, "I have something made for just you."

Temple described Freed getting up from behind his desk, opening his pants, and showing her his penis. Shocked, the innocent child responded with a nervous laugh that infuriated Freed, who yelled and demanded that she "get out" of his office. When Temple was reunited with her mother, her mother was upset and explained that MGM co-founder Louis B. Mayer had made sexual advances towards her, which prompted her to leave his office. Temple described the studio that produced "The Wizard of Oz" as a minefield for sexual child predators, saying it had "more than its quota of lecherous older men."

That was the beginning, and sadly, there has been no end.

Corey Feldman's experience as a child star in the 1980s was arguably worse than Shirley Temple's experience. Having starred in 1980s teen films "The Lost Boys," "The Goonies," and "Stand By Me," Feldman is one of the most vocal former child actors advocating against Hollywood's complicit support of pedophiles. After years of claiming that he and his late best friend, fellow actor, and co-star Corey Haim had been groomed and molested by men in the industry, he told their story in his 2020 tell-all documentary "My Truth: The Rape of 2 Coreys."

In the film, Feldman revealed that Haim confided in him that actor Charlie Sheen allegedly raped him in 1986 on the set of their film "Lucas" when Sheen was 19 and Haim was 13. Sheen and Haim's mother, Judy, denied the claim. Haim, who battled drug addiction and hardships, died of pneumonia in 2010.

Feldman is estranged from his parents. During an episode of Howie Mandel's "Howie Mandel Does

Stuff" podcast, Feldman implied that his parents were responsible for neglect that led to his abuse.

"My parents put me in the car with both pedophiles that abused me," he said. Though Feldman is an advocate for protecting children from pedophiles, he maintains his support of the late Michael Jackson, who has faced numerous child molestation allegations. Controversially, Jackson admitted to having young boys sleep in his bed when attending sleepovers at his house without their parents being present.

Jackson stressed that he did not have sexual relationships with the boys.

In 1993, Jackson was accused of sexually grooming three boys. Jackson faced charges of seduction, willful misconduct, sexual battery, and intentional infliction of emotional distress. However, the prosecutor decided not to file charges after the "primary alleged victim" reached an out-of-court settlement with Jackson--reported to be more than $10 million.

The other two boys actually supported Jackson's claim of innocence.

Wade Robson is a former child dancer from Australia who met Jackson when he was 5 after winning a Michael Jackson dance contest in Brisbane during the late 1980s before moving to Los Angeles. James Safechuck met Jackson when he was 10 and was selected to appear in a Pepsi commercial with Jackson. Both Robson and Safechuck provided witness testimony for Jackson in 1993. Robson also testified in support of Jackson in 2005 when the King of Pop's charges of molesting Gavin Arvizo went to trial.

However, both Robson and Safechuck changed their positions in 2013, saying they lied, according to NPR. Robson and Safechuck filed separate molestation suits against Jackson's estate in 2013 and 2014, respectively. While both suits were dismissed, Robson and Safechuck's accounts of being groomed and sexually assaulted by Jackson were the subject of the four-part 2019 HBO documentary, "Leaving Neverland."

After watching "Leaving Neverland," Feldman sustained his support for Jackson, but admitted that he identified with some of Robson and Safechuck's interactions with the entertainer who died in 2009.

Feldman said via Twitter: "All I know is what I experienced, and yes, every experience was the same.... right up until the sex part," Feldman shared. "That is where it becomes LaLa Land, instead of Neverland for me. We never spoke about sex other than a few warnings about how sex was scary, & dangerous... MJ never once swore in my presence, never touched me inappropriately, and never ever suggested we should be lovers in any way!"

Bad Boy Entertainment mogul Sean Diddy Combs came under fire for child grooming allegations in 2023, after his ex-girlfriend, singer and model Cassie Ventura sued him for sexually abusing her and forcing her to participate in "Freak Offs" with sex workers. Though Diddy settled the suit out-of-court within 24 hours, speculation of other alleged instances of sexual grooming began to mount. Old interviews with Diddy protege Usher Raymond resurfaced, suggesting that the "Yeah" singer may have been a victim of Diddy's sexual grooming of minors.

The 2024 halftime performer recounted Diddy exposing him to highly inappropriate sexual activities when he was 15 years old. At the time, Usher lived with the then 23-year-old Diddy for a year while Diddy executive-produced his self-titled debut album. Though there are no reports of Usher accusing Diddy of abusing him, the things Usher witnessed at the "Puffy Flavor Camp" sound similar to the Freak Offs described in the Diddy lawsuits.

During a 2004 interview with Rolling Stone magazine, Usher revealed that Diddy had introduced him to a different set of "shit--sex, specifically." Usher explained that women were always present and there was a lot of sex happening.

"You'd open a door and see somebody doing it," he said, recalling living in Diddy's house, "or several people in a room having an orgy. You never knew what was going to happen." Usher had sexual encounters with women while living in the house but claims he did not have intercourse until he was 19.

When appearing on "The Howard Stern Show" on SiriusXM in 2016, Stern and co-host Robin Quivers asked Usher about the "wild" time he spent at the Puffy Flavor Camp as a youth. While Usher made light of what he was exposed to while living in the house, he exclaimed, "Hell no!" when asked if he would recommend Puffy Flavor Camp to his children. In 2009, however, Usher did send Justin Bieber, his then 15-year-old protege and rising popstar, to spend forty-eight hours under the disgraced mogul's supervision.

The video footage of Diddy and Bieber discussing the plans for their two-day binge is an awkward exchange between the newcomer and the 40-year-old superstar known for his adult party lifestyle. "We're hanging out, and what we're doing, we can't really disclose, but it's a 15-year-old's dream. I've been given custody of him," Diddy says in the video clip. "I had legal guardianship of Usher when he did his first album. I don't have legal guardianship of [Bieber], but for the next forty-eight hours, he's with me. And we gone go 'full, buck fool crazy.'" A seemingly nervous Bieber plays along and says that he wants to go get some girls.

Despite Bieber's tremendous success over his 15-year career, he's also experienced some tough times, battling drug and alcohol addiction.

Since the Diddy sexual assault allegations emerged, there have been rumors that Diddy may have assaulted Bieber, but the "Baby" singer has not addressed the speculation.

Bieber has opened up about the struggles of being so young when he got his start in the industry during a 2020 interview with Apple Music's Zane Lowe. Bieber did not name any perpetrators in the music business, but he became emotional when asked about Billie Eilish, who was just 13 when she scored her first viral hit.

"It was hard for me being that young and being in the industry and not knowing where to turn and everyone telling me they loved me and just turn their back on you is just sad," Bieber said as he wiped tears from his eyes. "So, if [Billie] ever needs me, I'm going to be here for her. ... I just want to protect her. I don't want her to go through anything I went through. I don't wish that upon anybody. Yep. If she ever needs me. I'm just a call away."

Usher's mother and former manager Jonetta Patton admits she was hesitant to let her 15-year-old son leave their Atlanta home and move to New York to live with Diddy for one year.

Usher was signed to Kenneth "Babyface" Edmonds and Antonio "L.A." Reid's LAFace Records when he was 14. He appeared on the "Poetic Justice" soundtrack in 1993 but lost his voice due to puberty. Patton said his label deal was in jeopardy, and it was a business decision for Usher to be mentored by Puffy.

"I didn't know Puffy," Patton told *Today* in 2020. "I will never forget it. We had this conversation, and he said, 'You have to trust me.' That was a really, really hard decision.'"

Usher told The Howard Stern Show that his parents were not aware that he was exposed to orgies while living with Puffy. "They didn't know nothing about this shit," Usher said with a laugh. "I was having a good time."

But did Diddy breach Patton's trust?

The answer may be reflected in the advice Patton offers to parents of children in entertainment. "Stay with your kid," she told *Today*. "I don't care what they say because they tried to push me out. They didn't want me in. They would actually say, 'You're too close to the project. No, I'm not!'"

Patton's advice is consistent with the recommendations of other parents of children in Hollywood. Actress KeKe Palmer told Shannon Sharpe during her *Club Shay Shay* interview that her parents were always with her on television and film sets and spoke up to ensure she was treated properly. KeKe's mother, Sharon, later revealed to her that she was sometimes scared to speak up, but she had to protect her child.

When filming the movie "The Longshots" when she was 14, Ice Cube offered KeKe advice on avoiding predators. He told her to be careful.

KeKe recalls Ice Cube saying: "You are a beautiful young lady. And I see how nice you are, how kind you are to everybody on set. But I want you to know that you are growing into a young woman. A lot of times, the way people see you, the way these men see you on set, is not the way that you see yourself. So protect yourself. Be careful, and don't let them take advantage of you. Know who you are and know what you have so that people can't use it against you."

Former child actor and musician Drake Bell, who starred in Nickelodeon series "The Amanda Show" and "Drake & Josh," was not so fortunate. He was sexually abused by Brian Peck, who worked with Bell as the dialogue coach for "The Amanda Show."

Bell's devastating experiences are reflected in the Investigation Discovery five-part documentary "Quiet on Set: The Dark Side of Kids TV" which exposes dark behind-the-scenes stories of the Nickelodeon series during the 1990s and 2000s.

Peck met the profile of a child predator as described by the Department of Justice's national Project Safe Childhood initiative launched in 2006.

Peck groomed Bell by first targeting and isolating him. During the early stages of Bell's career, his father, Joe, was his manager. He accompanied his son to all of his tapings and always remained within earshot of his son. Joe was suspicious of the attention Peck was giving to his son and complained, but Peck's predatory behavior ensued.

Peck, however, used another manipulation tactic for grooming to seclude Drake. He convinced Drake and his mother, Robin Dobin, that Drake's father, with whom she was estranged, was mismanaging Drake's finances and was not a fit manager. Though these allegations were disproved, Joe was fired.

Peck stepped in to begin taking Drake to work, and sometimes Drake slept on Peck's couch when tapings ran late. This access to Drake was the gateway to Peck molesting the underage teen actor. Drake's mother was not aware of the abuse until the mother of Drake's then-girlfriend noticed Peck's controlling and stalking behavior towards Drake and informed Dobin. Dobin called the police, which ultimately led to Peck's arrest for eleven lewd acts with a child, including sodomy, sexual penetration by a foreign object, four counts of oral copulation, oral copulation by anesthesia or controlled substance, and using a minor for sex acts. A year later, Peck was sentenced to 16 months in jail. Despite the conviction, Peck continued to work on productions with child actors.

Ally Carter, a child human traffic survivor and outspoken activist who claims to have been used as a child sex slave at Diddy's freak-offs when she was a minor, has been speaking out about Diddy for four years.

Ally was not in her parents' custody when she was trafficked. She was in foster care.

In a live video posted on social media, Ally stressed that children need adult advocates to protect them from sexual predators.

"Kids need adults," she said. "Kids need somebody to be who they needed when they were a child. You know when you were saying something as a child and somebody said, 'Oh they just a kid. They don't know what they saying?' They need somebody to put they grown woman shit on and they grown man shit and do something."

Chapter Four: Deconstructing Brother Love

"Go ahead and hate your neighbor, go ahead and cheat a friend. Do it in the name of heaven, you'll be justified in the end." Excerpt from "One Tin Soldier," from the soundtrack of the film, Billy Jack.

Following Biggie Small's death, Sean "Puffy" Combs launched his own rap career, with the album *No Way Out.*

By the time he was preparing a second album, he had decided to make it a Christian rap album, and began referring to himself as a Christian, which was curious because signs of his transformation into a monster had already begun to show.

Diddy, the monster had begun to show, even before he tried to re-brand himself as "Brother Love."

Dr. Watts is an educator, father, husband, entrepreneur and cultural influencer. He is currently the CEO and co-founder of the Watts of Power Foundation, leading an initiative to recruit and train more Black male teachers. He earned his Doctorate in theology from Fuller Seminary.

According to Dr. Peter Watts, Jr., author of *Prodigal Father*, "Love, in its essence, is one of humanity's most profound and misunderstood forces. The Bible describes love in three distinct forms: eros, the romantic and often self-serving love; phileo, the love of friendship and camaraderie; and agape, the divine, unconditional, and sacrificial love epitomized by Jesus Christ. Each form has its place, but the confusion arises when eros disguises itself as phileo or agape."

"Sean 'Puffy' Combs, who once rebranded himself as 'Brother Love,' offers a metaphor for this phenomenon. In his artistry and persona, Combs often celebrated a love rooted in eros—passionate, indulgent, and self-focused. Yet, by adopting the name 'Brother Love,' he suggested a deeper, more sacrificial form of love. It's a compelling image, but one that invites theological critique: Is this transformation a reflection of agape love or eros masquerading as something greater?"

Dr. Watts also illustrated that when eros is mistaken for agape, it creates a love that appears generous but centers on self. This kind of love may perform grand gestures or claim noble intentions, yet it lacks the enduring selflessness and transformative power of true agape.

"Eros, while powerful, can be deceptive. It seeks fulfillment in desire and personal gratification, and when unchecked, it can blur into relationships and acts that mimic the care of phileo or the selflessness of agape. True phileo love invests in friendships for mutual growth, while agape love sacrifices for others without expectation of return. Jesus embodied agape love—healing the broken, loving the unlovable, and ultimately giving His life for the redemption of the world.

"For Sean Combs, the name 'Brother Love' could signify a desire to embody something greater than himself. But as Christians, we know that real love is not about rebranding; it is about dying to self and living for others."

According to Dr. Watts, who received his Master's and Doctorate in Theology from Fuller Seminary, Diddy initially came off as simply trying to brand himself.

"Initially it was cool, just branding and marketing. But his attempt in calling himself Brother Love was to brand himself as a person that is about world peace and trying to bring joyous love, friend love to the music industry to say that's what he wants to embody.

"As we see, it was a smoke screen for bastardizing what true love is."

Many Christians are wondering how Sean Combs could call himself a Christian while committing heinous acts against others.

"I guess it would be the same as people calling themselves Black when they're really not, said Dr.

Watts. "You can label yourself whatever you want, but it's about how you live it out.

"Throughout history, a whole bunch of people called themselves Christian but were anti-Christlike. Murder, pillaging and slavery were all done in the name of Christianity. Him calling himself 'Brother Love' is par for the course."

Dr. Watts added that committing evil acts and having the ends justify the means has been the mission for any number of people who call themselves Christians.

"When we think about systemic racism within Christianity and the way in which it operated, 'ends justify the means' is usually invoked. It's about a grab of power. That's what the Bible is about—we see what God intended, juxtaposed to what man chose to do.

"The Garden of Eden was a place where all was good. When God created man, he gave him access to everything except one thing and man chose that one thing anyway."

That event, "The Fall" is where it all started said Dr. Watts. That was the fall of the human condition and the beginning of the brokenness of humanity.

"Instead of worshipping the creator who created the thing, we would rather worship the thing—money. When you clamor to money and power, you will do anything it takes to get it.

"'Gladiator' was about clamoring to get power. Humanity will justify the means to get to the end. To grab hold to power, because a million isn't enough when I get it. I now need two million. However you got it, you got to keep doing it to keep it."

Dr. Watts calls it a "Crisis of Morality." He thinks that something was off while Diddy was developing his moral compass.

"Think about how he started in entertainment as an intern with Andre Harrell. There is no telling what he was introduced to in his early years in the music game.

"Imagine what his home was like with his mother. He was shaped and formed to be a particular way. Money and power only expose what is already inside of you. Money exposes whatever is already in your heart. Money and power can change all of us when we don't become content with what we acquire."

According to Dr. Watts, when it's never enough, that's when we get exposed.

"The Bible talks about being content.

"In my life, I don't have wants, I have needs and that's what I ask God for. We start with hundreds of needs, and we end up with millions of needs. Not that I want the money, I just need the resources. Once my needs are met, I'm good. I don't need everything."

Can Diddy be redeemed?

"Everybody can be redeemed. No one is above redemption. I don't have a hell to condemn them to or a heaven to send them to. There but for the grace of God…one bad decision for my life to crumble. I would want redemption if I'm contrite and trying to seek forgiveness and to make amends with those that I have hurt. There is always room for reconciliation.

"From Genesis to Revelations, when God created this world, it was good, and a decision was made that allowed for the brokenness.

"The story of the bible is not what we should do, but how we behave and make mistakes and even when becoming murderous, God never gave up on us. One was sent to fix what was broken and we all have the opportunity to be redeemed. I always want to be a part of that redemption story."

Part of being redeemed is showing contrition, and according to Dr. Watts, Diddy has shown none.

"We have to be contrite in asking for forgiveness and making amends with those we hurt. We saw the attempt when he apologized after Cassie's beatdown tape was broadcast across the world, and it was all theatrics. There is true repentance and that ain't it.

"Jesus calls us to move beyond the illusions of love and embrace its truest form: agape. This love is not a label or a persona—it is an action, a sacrifice, and a way of being that reflects the heart of God. Only when we live in agape do we experience love in its purest and most authentic form."

It may have sounded nice, and it may have appeared to be transformative, but Sean Combs trying to call himself "Brother Love," was a failure at making an appearance of being a loving person.

When Bad Boy Records lost its flag ship artist, Biggie Smalls, the search was on to find a replacement. Sean "Puffy" Combs became a solo artist, but that didn't fill the gaping hole left by the iconic artist.

Puffy discovered Shyne, a Belizean rapper who sounded very much like Biggie. And, just like with Biggie, Puffy pretended to be Shyne's friend.

In 1999, Shyne and Puffy were at a nightclub in NYC when a commotion started and three people were injured. Shyne was convicted of assault and unlawful possession of a weapon and sentenced to ten years in prison, after which he was deported back to Belize.

The rumor mill laid out a story of Puffy handing the gun to Shyne, promising to take care of his legal defense, only to later completely abandon him.

When Shyne was released, he and Puffy made their peace. But the former rapper bristled at Puffy calling him "brother."

"I wish I was his brother in 2000, when we were on trial. I wish I was his brother for the last 26 years when my mom never got any assistance. He never helped to dry her tears."

Combs hasn't been anything close to "Brother Love."

Sean Combs is a monster, and the opposite of Love.

Chapter Five: The Amorality of Entertainment

Why is there so much sexual perversion, coercion, abuse and outright exchange of sex for success in entertainment?

The answer isn't very complicated.

Music, television and film are forms of entertainment that are created to make people feel good with fantasy.

But for many, the fantasy dreamworld turned into a nightmare landscape of physical, mental and emotional abuse, as sexual deviance tethered itself to wealth and power, resulting in systematic sexual exploitation became as much a part of the entertainment industry as the talent being exploited.

When the entertainment industry started in the early 1900's, the abuse was rampant and not very many people opposed it openly, because of the money involved and laws that were unclear and mostly unenforced.

The abuse is so pervasive to the industry that part of what seems to be policy also seems to shield predators from allegations of sexual harassment and assault.

But since the 1980's, victims and advocates have been fighting back stronger and stronger, with emerging legal protections and more powerful advocacy.

A new report published by four US-based not-for-profit organizations called Sound Off "chronicles the scathing history and financial impact of decades of sexual abuse and cover ups in the music industry, from the 1950s to the present".

Sound Off calls on the music industry to implement measures to abridge sexual harassment and assault in the industry.

"For decades, the music industry has condoned, perpetuated and often marketed a culture of sexual abuse of women and underage girls", the report states. "Thousands of artists, executives and shareholders have made billions of dollars in profit – while engaging in and/or covering up criminal sexual behavior."

Sound Off "catalogues public information on reported sexual abuse, harassment and related misconduct involving musicians and music industry executives.

The report launches wider advocacy for victims and calls for the abolition of non-disclosure agreements (NDAs) that silence survivors.

Sound Off also calls for publishing the names of perpetrators "credibly accused of sexual assault and harassment," since disclosure has historically been difficult due to pressure from powerful abusers.

At an *Elle Magazine* Women in Hollywood event in 2017, Reese Witherspoon disclosed her sexual assault experience while she was still a minor.

"I have my own experiences that have come back to me very vividly. I have found it hard to sleep. So many feelings — anxiety about being honest, guilt for not speaking up, disgust at the director who assaulted me when I was only 16, anger that I was made to feel that silence was a condition of my employment. I wish I could tell you that it was only one incident.

"Sadly, I have had multiple experiences, and I don't speak about them very often, but after hearing these women tonight, being so open and honest, it has made me want to speak up. And I actually feel less alone."

Actress Jessica Chastain, at the same event:

"I had a producer spank me as I walked past him in a hallway. I didn't speak up, because I was worried that I might be made un-hireable by dissenting. I have stopped making myself invisible, or small, and to my shock and happiness, my career has not stalled.

"In speaking up, I've come to understand that if a director or a studio doesn't hire me because of my stance on wage equality, diversity, or sexual harassment, then I'm fine with that. This is an industry rife with sexism, racism, and homophobia. It's so closely woven into the fabric of the business that we've become snow-blind to the glaring injustices enacted every day."

Kathleen Kennedy, a film producer with more than sixty films to her credit, including Jurassic Park, The Sixth Sense, Rogue One, and The Girl on the Train, expressed a sense of responsibility to make real progress, even calling for the creation of a commission, created by the film industry to fight against sexual harassment and abuse within the industry.

"The organizations that constitute the American film industry — the studios, the unions the guilds and the talent agencies — should immediately convene a commission charged with the task of developing new, industry-wide protections against sexual harassment and abuse.

"The commission should be composed of specialists in labor and management practices, lawyers and legal scholars, sociologists, psychologists, feminist activists and theorists, as well as people who work in film and television. The commission should be fully funded by our industry in order to address the task at hand in a thoroughgoing, comprehensive fashion. The goal of this commission would be to transform our industry in regards to sexual harassment and abuse in the workplace.

"I've asked the Board of Governors of the Academy of Motion Picture Arts and Science, of which I'm a Governor, to take the first steps towards creating this commission. We have to act."

The root of Kennedy's call for the commission includes plentiful "terrible and terrifying stories about sexual harassment and assault in the film industry that have dominated the news…a demand is growing for action to prevent further civil and human rights abuses in the future.

"Increased awareness of the belittlement, objectification and predation long endured by women who work in film, will certainly be one result of the exposure of what Harvey Weinstein did, and was permitted to do; women who are subject to similar criminal treatment in the future will certainly look to the brave women who've come forward to tell what was done to them as these shocking and also horribly familiar events have been brought to light. The light of public scrutiny will have been strengthened, and we all hope the ability of corporations, board of directors, and colleagues to cover up and countenance sexual predators will be severely curtailed.

"Predators must come to feel that they can't count on power or wealth or fame to shield them from the consequences of their actions. But sexual harassment of women and men, predation, rape and the misogyny that is the context for this inhumanity will continue unless there is a decisive, industry-wide, institutional response that legislates change rather than hopes for it to happen."

That response should include some of the very people who are accused of sexual abuse.

Emory Andrew Tate III, professionally known as Andrew Tate is a former kickboxer who now creates content for the "manosphere." He was the third most googled person in 2023 and has labelled himself a misogynist.

Tate, who has battled charges of rape and human trafficking, addresses sexual perversion--the mainstay of the entertainment industry--explained why sexual perversions exist on his social media platform, *Hustler's University*.

"Please understand, all the artists you listen to, all the actors you like and all of the sports stars—the garbage people you follow, have sold their souls. They have done it for their own personal gain, so they can make millions, and they don't care how they damage society by extension.

"You are society. They have decided to damage you to benefit them.

"You're sitting at home jerking off to the Superbowl's halftime show and going to concerts, supporting the people who have sold you out. You need to sit as a human at home and ask: 'Am I going to idolize someone who has sold their soul? (Someone) who will tell my children bad ideas, because I like their music?'"

An often-overlooked element in sexual abuse has been the sexual assault of men and boys in the industry.

It took Terry Crews two years to finally begin speaking out about the issue as it relates to men and boys, when he opened up at the "Man Up: Unpacking Masculinity" panel at the *Teen Vogue Summit*. Crews spoke on the reasons why he broke his silence and decided to pursue legal action to hold his attacker accountable for crimes against Crews.

Crews alleges that in 2016, WME Agent Adam Venit molested him by squeezing his genitals at a party.

While Crews was embarrassed, the initial public reaction was to mock him, since he was so much larger than his assailant.

Even rapper Fifty Cents went on Instagram and mocked Crews, stating that he doubted if Crews could be assaulted because of his size.

"The truth was, I understand where he was coming from," Crews said. "If I would have picked [my attacker] up and threw him out the window, does that mean I wasn't assaulted? I'm still assaulted. The problem--this is the hard part--is that if I got assaulted, anyone could. And that's not acceptable."

Crews released WME as his agency in 2017, and then sued both the agency and Venit. Part of the settlement was for the agency to fire WME.

Not everyone who enters the entertainment business has problems with sex for play, sexual assault or even gets approached.

Alonzo "Lonzo" Williams started as a club promoter in the late seventies who made good money before deciding to enter the music industry. He was already an entrepreneur, so instead of going the traditional route of seeking a record deal, he started off by creating a record company of his own, Kru-Kut records, which included distribution, radio and promotions relationships.

Now known affectionately as the Godfather of West Coast Hip Hop, Lonzo is responsible for launching the World Class Wrecking Cru, which contained

Dr. Dre and led to the creation of N.W.A. Under the Wrecking Cru, Lonzo, Dre and Michel'le unleashed the legendary song "Turn Off the Lights."

Lonzo said that while he knew that there was some sexual abuse in the industry, it bypassed him. He never had a problem because "I never came off as an approachable person.

"It was obvious to people who met me that I was on some pussy. My primary motivation was to get my dick sucked."

Lonzo said that no women came at him with a hard offer either, which was just as well since he wasn't interested in sexual exchanges.

"I was able to dodge women a lot smoother," he said. "It wasn't about quid pro quo for me. But, with women, it was always a softer approach. I saw it coming and I never was seen with an ugly woman. If you saw me with an ugly woman, I was holding her for the police."

In addition, Lonzo, who had a major hit with Dr. Dre ("Turn Off the Lights") said that abusers look for a type.

"There is a type--the ones who come into the game with nothing but talent and desperation. I was never desperate, because I was an independent label owner all along. When I got the deal with CBS, I already had an album out. I already had radio relationships.

"As a new talent in entertainment, you just have your talent and a pussy. Or a bootyhole. If you fly into a city with no resources looking to get into entertainment, you are fresh meat. And just like a pimp who waits at the bus stop for new girls with no resources, there are people in the entertainment industry who are also waiting.

"It's the same game and it's easy. Fresh out of school smelling like desperation and you have nothing to fall back on. Then, here comes a person who can change the trajectory of your life with the swipe of a pen. You feel indebted to them, and everyone wants to get a bonus no matter what it is. You become the bonus for them."

According to Lonzo, being unaware and entering into unwritten deals where sex is exchanged is how people of influence with resources and no talent end up profiting off people who have talent but no influence or resources.

"Diddy is not a rapper! He can't (w)rap a gift if you put your finger on the bow. He could half ass dance, but he really had no talent, so he used the talent he found to put himself out there.

"He grabbed Biggie and Mary J. Blige. He used them and ended up hating them and had to make himself feel good. He had to make them feel subservient so he would have something over them—whether its sex or screwing them over in a deal."

Lonzo said that Diddy became a monster when the people he was using either decided to pull away from him or were planning to do their own thing. That made him vindictive.

"He's vindictive like Donald Trump. He will go after people at his own cost. Vindictiveness supersedes logic and everything else."

As for becoming a monster, Lonzo said that social media allowed Diddy to take everything to the next level, when he might have otherwise run out of gas after the 90s.

"I blame social media for a lot of shit. It allows people to present themselves in a manner that doesn't exist. He lived that life because he had money. He gave people something to aspire to be so they could get some trickle down, so they needed to be around him, and they would do anything, even though nothing ever trickled down."

After he was no longer making music, Combs used social media, along with parties featuring celebrities to maintain his allure.

"He used everyone, including the celebrities in his circle--Kim Kardashian, Jay-Z and Beyonce. If you were a regular person and got a ticket to that party, you could say that you went and hobnobbed with celebrities.

"He wasn't doing music anymore, but he was doing major deals with Cîroc and Sean John Clothing, with television and more. He represented an upper echelon of Hip Hop that no one in Hip Hop had achieved. He had so much of an aura of success that he did shit just to flex his power."

Believing his own hype, Puffy began to lose his grip, thinking that he was larger than he actually was and flexing his power more and more.

Part of flexing his power, said Lonzo, included taking Al B. Sure (Albert Brown)'s woman (Kim Porter) and adopting his kid (Quincy Brown).

"Diddy thought he was making people look stupid. And he was fucking everyone in business and in sex."

Lonzo explained that Diddy started believing his own hype because nothing was happening to him, even with all the wild things he was doing.

"He thought he was a black John Gotti calling shots. And if you wanted to be around him, you had to bring something...booty...pussy...

"He made himself feel better by making people do things they wouldn't normally do and then giving them a check or threatening them. He also made records about this as though he was untouchable and that will piss people off."

But that plan ran out when Homeland Security stepped in and shut everything down.

Lonzo said that someone got angry at Diddy and figured out a way to trigger the federal authorities' involvement.

"You have racism in the FBI and maybe even jealousy. Some regular agents making 80-100k don't like you, so they use a whole team of lawyers to come after you and they use you to make their career. When promotions come around, they hope to go from 80k to 120k.

"You don't know what triggers a person's downfall, but I think he got too obvious. That's what gets you shut down. When you do things blatantly and you make the authorities look like they aren't doing their job, you make them look weak. He was making the authorities look weak, because people had probably been calling the authorities on him forever, but he got too big and felt too big."

It could have been very simple, said Lonzo.

"Maybe he pissed off the parents of a young white girl who went through their country club rolodex and made complaints.

"I said this about Suge (Knight, head of Death Row Records, now imprisoned for a hit and run that killed one man and injured another in 2015)—his biggest mistake was standing in front of those two Rolls-Royces with all that red on the cover of *The Source*. He kept flaunting his wealth and being flashy.

A flashy black man is a target.

Chapter Six: East versus West

"Any artist out there that want to be an artist and stay a star, and don't have to worry about the executive producer trying to be all in the videos, all on the record, dancing... come to Death Row!" – Death Row's Suge Knight at the Source Awards.

Hip Hop is filled with legendary battles, from MC Lyte v Antoinette; LL Cool J v Kool Moe Dee; and from the Real Roxanne v Roxanne Shante to NWA v Ice Cube.

Some of those battles were of unknown origins.

Still other battles came from real problems rappers had with each other, including any given member of NWA, as the group splintered, losing first Ice Cube and then Dr. Dre.

Some Hip Hop beefs showed potential to get ugly, but in general, were resolved without any major incidents.

Until the war between Bad Boy Records and Death Row Records, which had many people convinced that there was a war between two entire coasts.

In a very short time in 1994, a rift between two rappers, Death Row's Tupac Shakur and Bad Boy's Notorious B.I.G., turned into an all-out war between their labels, Death Row Records and Bad Boy Records.

Contrary to bad reporting by mainstream media, and cult-like ignorance of industry minions and the general public, there was NEVER a war between the entirety of east coast rappers and west coast rappers. People tried to make it larger than it was, but it was between the two labels, sparked by two rappers and then two label owners.

Before there was any beef, Tupac and Biggie were friends. Sean John Combs, known as "Puffy" at the time was said to have been fond of Tupac and wanted his friendship, but rejection was swift and sure.

"Pac didn't have any kind of respect for Puff," Hip Hop photographer Monique Bunn told Rolling Stone Magazine, saying that Tupac viewed Puffy as a "corny executive," and Biggie as his peer.

Things "got blown out of proportion," according to Bunn, after Tupac was shot five times in a recording studio in New York in 1994. Tupac was certain that Puffy and personnel from his record label had set him up to be killed.

Tupac was known for recording "sides" (laying a verse on someone else's track) for other artists as a way of making extra money. Sides were typically paid for in cash, which meant that the artist didn't have to report the money to their record company or to the IRS.

On November 30, 1994, Tupac was in New York, recording a side for Little Shawn at Quad Studios. He was embroiled in a legal battle, accused of sexual abuse. The fee for the side was earmarked for his legal expenses.

When Tupac arrived at the studio, the rap crew Junior M.A.F.I.A. (affiliated with The Notorious B.I.G and signed to Bad Boy Records) were outside. He and the crew exchanged pleasantries and Pac entered the studio, to be greeted by two gunmen, shouting for everyone to hit the floor.

Tupac hesitated, and for that, the gunmen shot him five times and still robbed him.

On his way out of the building on a stretcher, Tupac saw B.I.G. and assumed he was set up. He gave B.I.G. and the crew the middle finger.

While still recovering, Tupac was convicted in his sexual assault case and sent to Riker's Island to serve out his sentence.

Even though Puffy visited Tupac in prison to assure him that no one affiliated with Bad Boy had been involved in the shooting, Tupac told *Vibe Magazine* that Biggie, Puff Daddy and Uptown Records head Andre Harrell were to blame for his attack at the studio and subsequent shooting.

That was the end of any friendship between Tupac and Biggie and the spark of the feud between Bad Boy Records and Death Row Records, Tupac's new recording home.

It was Death Row's CEO who chose to put up the legal and financial resources to get Tupac out of prison, after which he began to record for the label at breakneck speed.

In February 1995, "Who Shot Ya?," a B-side track from Biggie's "Big Poppa" single was released. Although Combs and Biggie denied having anything to do with the shooting and stated that "Who Shot Ya?" had been recorded before the shooting, Tupac interpreted it as a taunt directed at him.

"C'mere, c'mere ... open your fucking mouth ... Didn't I tell you not to fuck with me? ... Can't talk with a gun in your mouth huh?"—Notorious B.I.G., from Who Shot Ya?

When Biggie released the lyrics that seemed to mock Tupac's shooting, things heated up to a near raging fire.

On August 3, 1995, at *The Source Magazine's* annual *Source Awards*, Death Row's CEO climbed on stage and uttered these now legendary words: "Any artist out there that want to be an artist and stay a star, and don't have to worry about the executive producer trying to be all in the videos, all on the record, dancing… come to Death Row!"

Suge was mocking Puffy for inserting his ad-libs on Bad Boy artists' songs and shimmying throughout their videos.

The crowd, however, comprised of mostly New York artists and NYC Hip Hop fans, misunderstood Knight and took his dis of Puffy as a stab at their music as a whole. As a result, they booed Suge and then booed Dr. Dre when his award for Best Producer was announced.

Defending his mentor, friend and treasured producer, Snoop dug in on the crowd: "The east coast ain't got no love for Dr. Dre and Snoop Dogg and Death Row? Y'all don't love us? Y'all don't love us?! Well, let it be known then! We don't give a fuck. We know y'all east coast! We know where the fuck we at!"

The crowd did let their feelings be known, slowly turning from the boos to clapping for Snoop to show their love.

This writer also made a statement at *The Source Awards*.

While my magazine, *Rap Sheet* was a competitor for *The Source*, I remained friends with its founder, David Mays. Mays gave permission for my crew to pass out copies of *Rap Sheet* in the lobby at *The Source Awards* and he invited me to speak at the event. My message was one of conciliation.

I introduced myself and let the audience know that I was from the Midwest and had lived on the east coast before making the west coast my home. I told them that I had love for the east coast and asked if they had love for the west coast. It took a moment, but the audience warmed up and showed love through applause.

Not only was the alleged east coast versus west coast feud not inclusive of the entirety of both coasts, but not every person in either camp was a willing participant.

"They tried to get me to not like Puffy and Biggie while we was in the middle of the Death Row and Bad Boy feud," said Snoop. "I made a choice that I had no issues with them."

And, James Lloyd, professionally known as Lil Cease, claimed on Vlad TV, that it was Diddy, who was going by Puffy at that time, who moved to keep the feud from going ballistic.

"We didn't know about Suge and Puff having no issues," he said. Adding that earlier in the day the Bad Boy crew had come across Daz Dillinger (from the Dogg Pound) and Snoop Dogg and no problems were detected.

"Everything was all fine. We (were) thinking everything is all love," Cease continued. "It was other shit going on — Bone Thugs was beefing, I think, with Death Row at that time with the Eazy-E shit (Eazy had Bone on his Ruthless label, and was allegedly still getting paid from Dre, after the legendary producer started Death Row Records with Marion "Suge" Knight). But it was cordial and mutual with us. We didn't think nothing of the situation. Everything was all love until [Suge] got on that stage and said that shit."

Suge Knight's legendary statement was heavy hitting, indeed.

A west coast music mogul came to the east coast and made a derogatory statement about one of the leading rap music icons of New York. That was a bold and brash move and left more than a few jaws dropped.

"Everybody was looking at each other like, 'Huh? Really?' Shit could've went different in there," said Cease.

However, Cease said it was Puffy who advised the crew not to retaliate.

"Puff being Puff, [said], 'Nah. We not gon' go that route. We gon' let it be,'" Cease recalled.

The Junior M.A.F.I.A. rapper explained that it was Biggie's intent to clap back against Suge , but he took Puffy's advice to let sleeping dogs lie because he "really trusted Puff and took Puff's word."

"Like, nah, we not gon' go that route, and we kind of just let it be," he explained.

When it was time for Puff Daddy to take the stage, he was conciliatory.

"All this East and West—that needs to stop. So, give it up for everybody from the East and the West that won tonight. One love."

Lil Cease added: "we took it for what it was worth, like, we ain't really with that type of vibe right now. But Puff was the one who was responsible for putting Big at the position he was at, and for Big staying chill, staying down. And we kind of just let it be."

But things just weren't meant to just be left alone.

The following month, both Suge Knight and Puffy went to Jermaine Dupri's birthday party at Platinum House Club in Atlanta. The entourages for both men fell into conflict, and the conflict overflowed from the club to the streets and resulted in the death of Jai "Big Jake" Robles, a friend of Knight's. Big Jake was shot dead while getting into a limousine and Knight pointed the finger of blame at Combs.

Not too long after Big Jake's death, Knight secured Tupac's release with a bond of $1.4 million.

Upon his release, Tupac went to work recording music and hyping up the feud between Death Row and Bad Boy.

And, when Dr. Dre left Death Row, Tupac went after him with a vengeance, referring him by name as Alize, the fruity champagne popular in the 90s.

By 1996, the feud between the Hip Hop labels had fizzled out as first Tupac in 1996 and then Biggie Smalls in 1997, were gunned down, cutting their lives and their successful careers short.

Chapter Seven: Chasing Puffy

I wasn't the biggest fan of Biggie Smalls.

I liked his music. But I didn't really like him as a person.

My first encounter with him was having two young ladies coordinate a fashion shoot with him as the model.

Rap Sheet had a fashion feature called "On the Ragz" with clothing that designers would lend to us to place on artists as models. They would expect the clothing to be returned after the shoot. When the shoot with Biggie was over, he decided to steal the clothing and challenged them by asking them what they would do, since they were both females.

Ultimately, the designers told us to allow him to keep the clothing.

I was still hot.

But I didn't like it when I started hearing about how he was being treated at Bad Boy.

Apparently, his wife, singer Faith Evans didn't like it either.

that he drove Bad Boy Records as an artist, and didn't get to enjoy the spoils of his work.

In 1994, Faith Evans and Christopher Wallace, pka Biggie Smalls met one day at a Bad Boy photoshoot and married nine days later.

Friends and relations were cool with the union. Except one very important person—Big's mother, Voletta Wallace.

"He didn't want me and his mother to meet," Evans told The New York Post.

"She probably thought I was some groupie. But my daughter Chyna [then a toddler, from a previous relationship] was around quite a bit, and she saw the love I had for her. And the fact that I was a church girl and believe in the difference between right and wrong helped, too."

According to Faith, Biggie was struggling financially.

"The Christmas before his death, he needed to borrow $20,000, and he knew that I was the kind of person who would always be there for him, said Faith.

Faith Evans gave Big the money because she loved him, even though he was engaging with other women, primarily because she didn't have a jealous spirit.

"He wasn't even my man [Biggie was, by that point, fooling around with Lil' Kim and Charli Baltimore] — he probably took it and bought presents for his girlfriend! But I didn't care what it was for. He said he needed it, so I gave it to him."

But someone who did have a jealous spirit was Sean "Puffy" Combs.

Combs deceived the world into thinking that he and Biggie Smalls were the best of friends, but according to Bad Boy president, Kirk Burrowes, Puffy was in his feelings early on, when Tupac Shakur wanted nothing to do with Puff, but became close friends with Biggie

"There was someone on the sidelines, jealous," Burrowes said, referring to Combs.

It seemed that Puffy was jealous of Big's success and tried to keep up with him by centering himself in all of his artists' videos. Perhaps his jealousy ran so deep, he wanted to replace his flagship artist. With himself.

When Biggie died, Burrowes said that *Rolling Stone Magazine* wanted to do a cover and cover story on Biggie, but Puffy did everything possible to replace Biggie on the cover with himself.

"I was telling Sean, 'Let's make it Biggie. You still have a chance [for a cover in the future].,' said Burrowes.

He's like: 'No, he's dead. I'm putting out [Combs' debut album *No Way Out*] in July. I need to be on the cover of *Rolling Stone*.

And Puffy used his so-called friend's death to launch his own rap career. His debut solo song, "Missing You," was all about Puffy--not really about his so-called friend.

Nor was anything after Christopher Wallace's death about anyone else.

Biggie died broke.

There was no legacy of cash or assets from his music career to leave behind.

Even though Sean John Combs promised Voletta Wallace that he would take care of her and give her Biggie's publishing, he never did.

I didn't understand how an artist that had sold millions of records could be broke while his music was still hot.

So, I decided to interview Sean John "Puffy" Combs and ask him to explain.

We contacted his publicist and were assured that a telephone interview would be arranged since Puffy, and the Bad Boy artists were on tour. But that never happened. The publicist even told me that Puffy wasn't reachable on the tour bus because no one had a cell phone.

Puffy literally made a song about having money "hanging out our anus," yet no one had a cell phone on the tour bus?

However, weeks passed by, and my deadline was approaching, so I decided to fly to the cities where the Bad Boy crew was performing. I couldn't find the hotel where they were staying, and I couldn't get back stage.

It was clear that he was avoiding me.

While in a few cities, I did interviews with local radio stations. I let Puffy have it. I talked about how he was a coward to keep avoiding me. I gave my theories on why and that stirred things up a bit.

I chopped it up with Ryan Cameron in Atlanta and that made other stations want to interview me.

In New York City, I was scheduled to do an interview with Dr. Dre & Ed Lover on their show on Hot 97.

But that's when I learned how much money was being spent by Bad Boy Records and Arista Records on radio.

When I arrived at the station, and called upstairs, I spoke directly to Ed Lover, who greeted me and welcomed me to NYC—even though I had been there many times.

He informed me that he and Dre would welcome me with open arms, with one caveat. They had been told that if I came upstairs and did the interview, they would have to leave the building with me. So, he asked me if I would be able to hire them.

I knew he was joking about me hiring them. But I knew that there would be some real trouble if I did the interview.

I thanked him for the opportunity and the honesty and told him I was suddenly ill and wouldn't be able to come up.

But still no interview with Puffy for *Rap Sheet*.

Angered, exhausted and exasperated, I decided to use my media instrument to make my own statement.

I wrote a cover story in *Rap Sheet*, December 97, Vol. 6, No.1. I used the goofiest picture I could find to go on the cover.

The title of the story was: "Puffy: Why Is This Man on The Mic?

I wrote about how corny he was and about how he was taking Hip Hop backwards with his flavorless, talentless music as a solo artist.

But I also talked about how his whole method of success was to cheat his artists, including Total, Ma$e and The Notorious B.I.G.

And, I wrote and published my desire to "beat the shit out of him."

I ended the piece with this:

"I've taken inspiration from an interlude on Common's album *One Day It'll All Make Sense*, in which his father calls to say that he wants to set up an exhibition boxing match so that he can kick Jesse Jackson's ass.

"That's what I want to do" I wrote. "I want to create an exhibition boxing match between myself and

Sean "Puffy" Combs. I want to get Puffy in the ring before the world and his fans and kick his ass.

"I'm so upset over his dilution of rap music that I just want to beat the shit out of him. I could never catch him on the street and challenge him man to man, because his bodyguards are too deep, his lawyers are too powerful and I'm too far above meaningless public brawling anyway.

"So, I want to do the exhibition match with Puffy, live via pay-per-view. The proceeds should go to charity, but there are personal particulars at stake for us both: If I lose, I'll pen his autobiography and spin the greatest yarn, praising his accomplishments to his complete dictation. When he loses, he simply has to put down the mic

"Silly rabbit, tricks are for kids, and the microphone is for grownups."

After the magazine hit the streets, I was getting calls asking me if I would be afraid to travel to New York, since Puffy was now aware that I had beef with him and that I wanted to fight him.

I wasn't trying to be a tough guy, but I wasn't afraid of living my life the way that made sense to me.

That included standing up to any and everyone.

My motto has been "When I run, I run alone," for a very long time.

I was in NYC to interview an up-and-coming rap act, but when I arrived, they weren't there. My friend Glen Bolton, pka Daddy-O, from the group Stetsasonic, was there instead.

Daddy-O told me that the group and their manager were afraid to meet with me. He said that Puffy told them I was one of the biggest gangsters on the west coast. Daddy-O wasn't afraid of anyone, so he told them he would meet with me.

They weren't the only ones who had been told that about me.

Hilarious!

When I spoke to my second Confidential Diddy Source (CDS2) for this book, he said that I was very lucky things were different back then, and lucky he didn't have some of the relationships he has had in recent years.

"You're a lucky man. Things could have been very ugly if some of the people I know now were with him back then. These aren't good people and he loves to threaten people or more. He thinks he can do anything he wants, but that's why he's going through all he's going through right now.

"The chickens are coming home to roost."

CDS2 explained that over the past fifteen to twenty years, Diddy has had some shady characters coming around him to "handle" problematic situations.

"I've been hearing about how Diddy wants to call shots like a mob boss, so he has had people to act as 'enforcers.'"

Sean John Combs has been out in the world thinking he was a character from the underworld.

Attorney Ronda Dixon said that Puffy "got away with so much shit, he started thinking he was a gangster."

The biggest thing Combs got away with, according to Dixon, was stealing The Notorious B.I.G. away from the person who originally held his recording contract. That man was incarcerated and was Dixon's client at the time.

"I can't say the name because of attorney/client privilege, but someone who was incarcerated on RICO charges showed me the original contracts. Puffy was supposed to pay twenty thousand dollars of his legal fees, which he did not do."

Instead of paying the money, Puffy decided to stiff him and then ignore him, after securing Biggie Smalls as his artist for Bad Boy Records.

"Puffy just stopped talking to him. I didn't do anything as his attorney, because I didn't want to get involved.

"It's the same thing Suge Knight did with Harry-O, who put up the money for him to start the record company with Dr. Dre. Suge was supposed to be the proxy, that's why it was called 'Death Row Records,' but he never (settled his debt)."

Puffy burned his investor. That's not the only person he burned, and those things come back to haunt you.

I chased Puffy in the nineties.

The feds were chasing him in 2024.

His bullshit finally caught up to him.

Chapter Eight: The Night That Biggie Died

Death Row was having a hard time rebuilding after Dre left and Tupac died, and then Snoop made his way off the label and on to Master P's No Limit Records.

Bad Boy Records was still going strong.

Until Biggie was gunned down on March 9, 1997, less than one year after the shooting death of Tupac Shakur.

All sorts of rumors flew about both deaths.

The leading rumor at the time was that Puffy had placed a hit on Shakur and the wrong person shot him. When that man came to collect, Combs refused to pay. Subsequently, the alleged shooter issued an ultimatum to Puffy that if he didn't pay the hit fee, that he would be killed himself.

And, a huge story, which a number of people inside of Sean John Combs' circle corroborate, is that Combs had Biggie killed to prevent him from leaving Bad Boy Records and taking his royalties with him.

Biggie had proven to be a cash cow for Combs—especially since he wasn't receiving a fair share of royalties from his own music sales.

The only way he could get out from under Combs was to finish his contract with Bad Boy and start over somewhere else.

Biggie reportedly had plans to leave Bad Boy shortly before he died, Photographer Monique Bunn told *Rolling Stone*. "I know for a fact [because] he told me that," she said.

The night that Big was killed, there were too many specifics that were off, including the fact that he was supposed to be in London and Puffy convinced him to come to LA for the Vibe Magazine event.

Most interesting was the lack of proper security that night.

Puffy had lost security personnel along the way, including Anthony "Wolf" Jones, who was killed in an altercation in Atlanta, which CDS1 attributes to a dispute over a love triangle involving Puffy's girlfriend Kim Porter.

Gene Deal was security with Puffy for a while, including the night that Biggie Smalls was killed. He recounted that night on the *PBD Podcast*, with host Patrick Bet-David.

"We were cool, and we were going places and doing things...up until the night Big died...got murdered."

Deal used the word "murder" because, as he has asserted on multiple occasions, he believes that Puffy set the rapper up to be killed.

Deal didn't feel good about being in LA or about being in the city with less bodyguards than normal.

To top off the dread, Deal said he got a mysterious phone call that same day.

The caller issued a brief warning. This warning was: "They're coming to get y'all."

Deal was worried. The original plan for traveling to LA was to keep close to the hotel and just go to the *Vibe Magazine* event.

"When me and Puff touched down in California, we were going everywhere. We were going to the movies, the House of Blues—everywhere."

Worried, Gene Deal called the head of Bad Boy Records, Kirk Burrowes, to complain that the initial plan of laying low had changed. Deal was also worried because he was the only security personnel.

"Kirk, it's just me and him (Puffy) and the driver." Burrowes assured him that things would be alright and that he would be out in LA shortly.

But Deal was still uneasy, because of a call from a man named Wainsworth "Unique." Hall.

Unique "was a drug kingpin," said Deal.

"He called me and said: 'vest up.' And the phone hung up.

"I told Kirk that we needed more security. He tells me that Puff is not getting any more security."

My Confidential Diddy Source #2 (CDS2) recalled that he was supposed to go to LA and be on hand with Deal for Puffy and the rest of the Bad Boy artists. Instead, he got a call two days before and was told that he wasn't needed.

"That didn't make sense to me," said CDS2. "They were all travelling to LA for the *Vibe Magazine* event, so I knew they needed more security, not less."

According to Deal, "Big wasn't supposed to be in Los Angeles. (But once he arrived), I told Kirk Burrowes (that) we needed more security."

While Deal didn't tell Puffy about the call from Unique, he thought Puffy understood that LA was heated for Puffy, Biggie and the entourage.

He was also concerned because he remembered that Biggie made a phone call while the Dogg Pound was in NYC making a video and the video set got shot up.

Gene Deal was understandably worried about reprisal.

And, finally, Deal understood that Tupac may have been killed by a Crip, and since Puffy was rolling with the Crips, there may be problems with people who thought Puffy had something to do with Tupac's death.

Deal thought the simple solution was to add more security, so he went to Puffy's hotel to tell him what he thought. He thought that Puffy would be alarmed.

Instead Deal said that Puffy replied: "I don't want to hear that shit. If you don't want to go, don't go."

Deal left the hotel and went outside, where he saw Notorious B.I.G. They briefly spoke about Big's horrible contract with Puffy. Puffy came outside and they all went to the Peterson Museum, the venue of the *Vibe Magazine* event.

The growing tension between Puffy and Big was nearly palpable.

According to Deal, everyone knew Biggie was unhappy and looking to leave Bad Boy. And, he said that everyone knew that Biggie was finished with his album that he was preparing for his new record deal.

"Puff knew it too.

"Clive Davis and (Arista) had spent a lot of money to make Big a superstar. If someone else had written up a contract from another record label, like Capitol or Atlantic, who do you think they will tell first?

"They would tell (the other record label executive) 'your boy is coming over here (and) he's bringing us six groups."

According to Deal, Biggie already had a deal in place to have his own record label with himself as the main artist, but also including Lil Kim, Lil Cease and Cam'Ron.

Puffy was not happy about Biggie Smalls leaving Bad Boy to establish his own entity, so Deal said Puffy made moves to keep Biggie around him. While Biggie was supposed to be in London, Puffy made sure he was diverted to LA instead.

Deal said that Puffy had some ulterior motives for having Big on deck that night, which played out as the night progressed.

According to CDS2, "two inside people knew that Puffy wanted Biggie killed.

"Two different, reliable people told me that Puffy had tried to convince Biggie to stay with him and Bad Boy Records. He even offered to give him his publishing for the albums he already made for Bad Boy, and to give him a better deal moving forward.

"But Big was already done with Puffy and he was done with being just an artist. He wanted his own label and he wanted his freedom."

CDS2 recalled that Biggie was having some serious financial problems, and that "His new label was going to solve everything for him.

"He was about to have his whole life improved with the money he was getting from his new record deal. He was going to change his people's lives too.

"But Puffy didn't want anything to change. And if he couldn't keep him (on Bad Boy Entertainment), he was willing to take his life."

At the hotel, Gene Deal recalled that he was preparing to move Biggie and Puffy to the *Vibe Magazine* event.

"I went downstairs and got both vehicles—Biggie's car and our car (Deal and Puffy).

"We were going slow because Big could barely walk."

Biggie had a leg injury that was exacerbated by his weight. He was moving around in a wheelchair, said Deal, but he didn't want anyone to see him like that, so he would walk slowly with a cane.

The crew was supposed to be going to another party at someone's house. Deal, still feeling uneasy, called Chaz Williams from the Black Hand Mob, the security outfit he was with and let him know that "things are looking really shady here.

"What good would it do to tell Puffy that?"

Puffy decided they would go anyway.

According to Deal, Puffy wanted him to jump in the vehicle before he could secure both vehicles. Deal told the driver in Puffy's vehicle to run through stoplights, and he did. Two cars were moving together, but the car with Big wasn't moving and someone saw a gun being pointed at him.

Deal recalled: "I go to open the door and I hear something go "pop, pop, pop."

Biggie Smalls had been shot and the vehicle that the shots came from disappeared. For some reason, neither the cops, the fire department nor an ambulance responded.

Deal said that a local LA rapper, DJ Quik walked by and was saying: "I think they got one of them Bad Boy niggas. They said they was gonna get them."

Deal said that instead of taking Big to a hospital that was literally five minutes from where they were, they took him to a hospital thirty minutes away.

Not understanding the delay, Deal made it clear that they shouldn't allow Big to go to sleep.

"Do not let him go to sleep. Keep him up."

Deal pleaded with Biggie to stay awake so that he would have a better chance at survival.

He told him to hang on until they could get medical care.

The last words Biggie said were: "Just do it."

On March 9, 1997, Christopher Wallace, also known as The Notorious B.I.G. took his last breath.

To this day, despite promises to do so, Sean John Combs never delivered Biggie's royalties to his mother.

Biggie Smalls was legendary to many in the Hip Hop community.

For those who loved him most, the night he died was the night that Hip Hop stood still.

Chapter Nine: Becoming the Monster

"I was f---ed up. I mean I hit rock bottom, but I make no excuses. My behavior on that video is inexcusable. I take full responsibility for my actions in that video,"–Diddy, responding to a 2016 video of him assaulting Cassie Ventura, that surfaced in 2024.

When Casandra "Cassie" Ventura launched her suit against Diddy, shock and awe rang through the entertainment industry and the world.

There were rumors about Diddy being a monster, and a lot of people had stories, but Cassie suing Diddy made it real.

And, in 2024, when the tape from the Century Plaza Hotel in Los Angeles was released, it was clear that Sean John Combs was a monster.

That tape showed him savagely beating and kicking Cassie and there was no way to dress it up or cover it up.

Sean John "Diddy" Combs had become a full-fledged monster.

Either he started as a regular guy and became a monster, or he was fooling the world and was a monster from the very beginning.

According to Attorney Ronda Dixon, "Puffy wasn't always a man who would do dangerous things to people.

From the time she knew him in the early 1990's, Dixon didn't see him as a monster, or even a bad boy, like the name of his record company.

"What did Puffy do to become a 'bad boy?' Back then, nothing really."

But over the years, Combs showed himself to be more and more of a bad boy, a bad person, a monster.

Dixon knows about some of Diddy's most diabolical pursuits, because she has spoken to some of his victims.

"Albert Brown, (professionally known as R&B singer Al B. Sure!), is mad at Puffy for trying to kill him. Jamie Foxx also said that Puffy tried to kill him—for talking with loose lips."

And, according to one of my confidential sources, Diddy was trying to get people to keep their mouths shut, even as he was on the last days of his freedom.

Whether he was a monster all along, or developed into a monster, by the time the federal charges were coming down, Diddy started coming unhinged.

"Before Diddy was arrested, he started making threats," said the source.

"He was calling to tell people that testifying wasn't healthy for them.

"He was also visiting people with the same message."

One of those visits was to Usher Raymond's home. The result was that Usher called the police. The actual 911 call is available and is all over the internet.

Because Puffy had been acting like he was some larger-than-life gangster, some people who have stories to tell are afraid to tell them.

In fact, my primary confidential source would only tell his stories under the condition that he be anonymous.

I'll call this source "Confidential Diddy Source #1," or CDS1 For short.

CDS1 is a former football player, so he has a presence. His security career began in the marines, where he was doing security for club owners in the Philippines.

"That's about the same time that the early rappers were out like Whodini and Jekyll & Hyde (which contained the Executive of Uptown Records, Andre Harrel).

People wanted all the latest music in the clubs. DJs were like celebrities and needed protection, along with the clubs. People would get hyped up and I kept them from going too far.

"They would ask me to go with the club owner when he took money to the bank."

After his time in the marines, CDS1 landed in Atlanta, doing security for a mall and for housing developments.

He worked with other former football players who had started a security company in Atlanta, called Big Boy Security. Working with that company placed him in the company of Gene Deal, Diddy's bodyguard, who took over after Diddy's first bodyguard, Anthony "Wolf" Jones, was killed.

"That security company had me protecting people like Bowlegged Lous and working VIP sections."

Working with Gene Deal also placed CDS1 in the company of Sean John "Puffy" Combs.

"Puffy moved to Atlanta and I would be brought around when he had a big party in the ATL. He was working on opening Justin's (the restaurant named after Puffy's son). I spent time with him in the clubs.

"I worked for the owner of Dean Gardens where Puffy liked to do his parties, then called 'the Pajama Jammy Jams.'

"Wolf was with Diddy and we bumped heads initially because I was only concerned about the property. Diddy was renting the property to party. Wolf asked me to join his security team for Bad Boy."

CDS1 joined the security team for Bad Boy, so he got to know Puffy, who started asking him to go with him when he would move around town.

"Puffy knew me from working with Dean Gardens and the clubs, so he asked me to go around town with him. I was able to work the parties, even though I couldn't work for him specifically."

CDS1 recalled that one of the first incidents he had to manage involving Puffy was a violent incident involving Wolf, members of the Black Mafia Family (also known as BMF a crime-related organization founded in Detroit, Michigan in the mid-1980s), and Kim Porter, who ended up in a relationship with Puffy.

"Wolf was approached about a woman (Kim Porter) who he claimed as his girlfriend. She was also dating Puffy. BMF didn't like the way Wolf was dealing with the young lady, so they had a brief run-in."

CDS1 said that the run-in happened because someone from BMF was also interested in Kim Porter and one night, everything went awry.

"Wolf walked the lady to her car in the back of the club. There were shots in the air. The lady drove him to his car. Some of the BMF guys were just off property smoking. Someone in that group said something to Wolf and he barked back but kept going and got in his car. I saw a car drive through the property with no lights on and then I heard several pops and then, automatic gunfire. I saw the car fly by, still without lights. I saw someone lying on the ground.

"It was Wolf. He was half in the car and half out. I saw him lying there and I asked if he was alright, but there was no response.

"The car with no lights had been waiting the whole time and they got him.

CDS1 said that the fire department arrived first, with the police department arriving ten minutes later. He said someone claimed that the police deliberately delayed their arrival, but after the first police car arrived, other police cars started coming in by the droves from all directions.

"They say it was over some bad business, which could be true. But myself and Gene Deal--we believed that it was over that girl (Porter).

"What was also said was that Puffy held up a bottle and BMF held up bottles before it all happened."

CDS1 said that BMF had been hanging around because they had a relationship with Puffy. They would attend the Pajama Jammy Jams and even stay for the after parties, which were wild sex parties that ended up being the infamous "Freak Offs."

Toasting to someone's demise is indeed monstrous.

Chapter Ten: Puffy & The Freak Offs

Before I launched the second largest rap music publication, *Rap Sheet*, I was writing for a number of music media outlets, including *The Source* and *The Hip Hop Countdown & Report*, a nationally syndicated rap radio show.

As a freelance music journalist, I met and/or interviewed more than a handful of rap music icons, including Russell Simmons.

I would travel to New York City frequently since a good majority of the music industry business was located in that city.

While in New York, I would go to Simmons' office, or meet him at his favorite club, Nell's, in Greenwich Village.

I would see other writers and sometimes, recording artists at Nell's.

Eventually, Simmons invited me to a private party at a mansion.

I would typically roll alone, but for some reason, I decided to take a young lady I was dating.

When I arrived, I was glad that I did. She was the only woman in the house. But she was not the only feminine person in the house.

I looked around and saw Simmons and a few other people I knew, including the late Andre Harrell, President of Uptown Records and record executive, talent manager and television producer, Benny Medina, the real-life Fresh Prince of Bel Air.

Everyone was cordial. As the night went on, a couple of people were becoming touchy feely. Not so much with me, but I could see that some people were uncomfortable.

I knew that it was getting to be a good time to leave when things began to change. The lights began to dim, and some people seem altered as though they were under the influence of more than alcohol.

I looked at my date and she nodded her head. She could feel it too.

I heard the next day from an industry executive that the party turned into something that I wouldn't want to be a part of. He told me that it was a good idea that I had left.

Over the years, I received invitations to private parties, and I declined nearly all of them, because I had heard about some of the things that went on and I wanted nothing to do with any of the weirdness.

Attorney Ronda Dixon recalled that there were always parties going on in the music industry, but she was turning down any and all after-hour parties. She was also telling people off, including Diddy.

"I didn't go to any of them Freak Offs. (But) I told him off a long time ago—at the Jack the Rapper Convention. He was walking around with his son, and he had him in saggy diapers with a gold chain around his neck that had a gun and a naked woman hanging from it.

"I told him that he should be ashamed to do that to a child.

"I wasn't thinking about him doing anything to me. That's when he was a punk. Now, he's acting like 'Billy Badass.' He wasn't going to do anything."

Dixon said that Puffy wasn't the first to do wild parties with naked women.

"Luther 'Luke' Campbell was one of the first and he taught Puffy. He had a thing in the hotel ballroom at Jack the Rapper in Atlanta. He would rent a boat to go in the harbor in New York at the New Music Seminar. He had mentors.

"Clive Davis (head of Arista Records) would do those parties and have his 'boy toys' with him all the time. He was the only one to give Puffy a music company deal. No one else wanted to give Puffy a deal, because Andre Harrell (CEO of Uptown Records) sued him for the artists who should have been on Uptown.

Confidential Diddy Source 1 (CDS1) worked around Diddy for years and observed private parties that turned into even more private affairs. He believes that while some of the private parties had no name, that they were in fact, Freak Offs.

"Here is what I believed and what I know: the private parties were the Freak Offs," said CDS1. "You had to be somebody to get in there. No one back then called it a Freak Off.

"When Freaknic came to Atlanta, that might have been when people began referring to Puffy's afterparty as a Freak Off."

What exactly was a Freak Off?

"What was it? The only thing I could say I saw was more of oral sex in the open. You had to go behind the doors to see and do anything more than that. If you weren't invited, you couldn't be there, but you could pay your way in. You had to pay for membership, and it wasn't twenty-five dollars.

"I saw girls from the clubs doing oral to get their money in front of thirty people—they didn't care. In private rooms, I saw more than oral, but again, people were hiding their faces and most of the actual sex was doggy style. People didn't want to be identified.

"Most of them were probably strippers, but some I hadn't seen in the strip club—they were girls who were just open. Some went to the bathroom; some would cover their heads with a towel."

CDS1 said that most of the rooms had no doors, so that everyone could see what everyone else was doing.

"You had to do what everyone else was doing, so everyone was complicit."

CDS1 spent most of his time at doorways, because "that's where the issues were.

"Guys would be angry that their 'girl' was inside, but so were they. I would see dudes doubling and tripling up on one woman. Single men weren't allowed. Some guys would bring their girlfriends who would be in a room getting done by everyone.

"You had to bring a girl with you and have membership. You couldn't watch and not be a participant. You had to have a violation since you would see other people violating. Some men would have a female escort with them to get in and some guys would bring women they were in relationships with. Eventually, they would bring working girls who wanted their money up front."

The working girls, aka prostitutes didn't always work out because they wanted money up front, but the rules dictated that they had to perform first.

"Some women would come inside and decide they didn't like it or didn't like the men and wouldn't perform. Sometimes it would turn violent, so we were there to secure things.

"There were a lot of young people in there and some of them I didn't know. There were a lot of up-and-coming artists who weren't high value. This was early 90s. mainly, there were athletes."

The highest profile people in Atlanta at that time were athletes and strippers, because the strip clubs were very popular. Magic City was a strip club that was popular all over the states.

The strip club was gaining popularity in the south and the southeast in the 1990's, largely due to Luther "Luke" Campell, whose 2 Live Crew stage show included strippers, some of whom would dance in varying stages of nudity.

CDS1 worked the private parties thrown by Puffy, but he was still working strip clubs.

"I saw a woman who I had known since she was a child, and here she is in the strip club, working. She didn't want me to tell people I knew her.

"Regular everyday hard-working people would get out for lunch and come to the Magic City for lunch. They had a chef inside and vendors outside would grill. There were trucks barbecuing. They would come in the early afternoon, and the girls would start early. They also had students who went to the culinary school come in to cook at the club. I wanted to work more in the clubs, but they already had regulars who wouldn't give those spots up.

"But I still had my relationship with the owner of Dean Gardens, where Puffy rented apartments to do his private parties.

"I worked specifically for Dean himself. It was right outside of Atlanta. That place hosted everything."

The Atlanta-based event called Freaknic, an impromptu city-wide open party in the streets, influenced Puffy greatly, according to CDS1.

"Everything was freaky. The songs were all freaky. The people were so wild during Freaknic, that they were freaking on the streets of Atlanta. Some of the women were wearing miniskirts and panty hose that were crotchless, so that people could literally have sex on the streets, on vans, in cars..."

But by the late 1990's, Freaknic was under attack.

"The new mayor (Bill Campbell) the new prosecutor and new judges went back and prosecuted people. Then people were suing individuals. The lawsuits started when the videos started hitting the public.

"They were wilding out and thought they were anonymous, until twenty years later, when the videos started leaking on the internet—especially when the Freaknic documentary came out. That's when the lawsuits began."

Once Freaknic went away, Puffy's Freak Offs were more in demand.

"Everybody I knew in the music business showed up. Any given party could have Xscape, Lil G, Usher and his little brother were there. I had an issue with them because they weren't old enough to be drinking. Monica came through. She was still in her teens, but she got wilder as she got older."

Atlanta Powerhouse producer Dallas Austin was also there, CDS1 said, because he was in a relationship with Monica.

"Dallas had this superior attitude. He wanted to order people around and he wasn't paying anyone's salaries at these parties."

Another Atlanta-based super producer would attend Puffy's parties, but he would just show his face and leave.

"Jermaine Dupri was at every event. Everything in the city, Jermaine came in on it. He would show his face, pay his respect and then roll out. He wouldn't stay long. (Rapper) Da Brat came through before people knew she was gay.

"Toni Braxton came through a couple of events. These were high end events, but they still ended the same way. They would clear out the space and some people would either stay or come back. That's when the Freak Offs would start. Now, Toni is freaky. but there isn't anything that anyone could prove.

"When he had those kinds of events, most of the female artists with names wouldn't come to those. It was mostly guys and a bunch of strippers."

According to Confidential Diddy Source #2 (CDS2), the Freak Offs were diabolical and unsafe for women. This source didn't want any of his background details to be revealed, because he feared that he could be easily identified.

"The women who came to these parties thought that they were going someplace safe because of who was doing the parties.

"They would ask themselves: 'What could happen? Diddy won't do nothing to me.' But they were wrong."

CDS2 recalled going to Freak Off parties and seeing women who were "regular nice girls" get turned out.

"Some of these women I knew because of what I did for work. They were mostly rappers, singers, models and dancers. Some of them had recently moved, thinking they would have a chance to change their lives. They would come to these parties thinking they would meet someone who could help with their career. Things would start off cool, but then I would see them bent over butt naked or getting their mouths full of stranger dick."

CDS2 said that he would try to talk some of them out of going to the parties or out of staying late, but they thought they knew more than he did.

"I would see nice girls come to the Freak Offs with tiny tops and half of their asses hanging out. I knew how people would look at them and I knew what would happen. I would try to tell them what the parties were about, but they thought they were smarter than me.

"I remember seeing a girl I knew. I knew her family and I knew she was young. She might have been eighteen, but barely. I pulled her to the side and told her to take her ass home, but she got mad at me. And later that night, she was getting passed around like a blunt."

CDS2 said that the girls weren't all there to have sex, but they were young and naive, and there were a lot of drugs involved.

"I knew that drinks were getting spiked, and I had heard that the baby oil being used had the 'date rape drug' in it. I didn't see it for myself, but I saw the results, which was women doing things that they wouldn't normally do. It was hard to witness what they were doing knowing that somebody gave them drugs."

A "date rape drug" is the term given to drugs including Rohypnol, a hypnotic compound also called a "roofie."

The drug is usually given to someone secretly with the intent to render them unconscious and unable to function well enough to protect themselves against assault, which is usually sexual assault. The drug has been associated with acquaintance rape to the point where it is commonly called the "date rape drug."

CDS2 explained that the usage of drugs was the only way to explain why the young girls and even some men would be nearly unconscious and doing wild things with strangers.

"I made sure that I didn't drink anything, and I made sure that I wasn't alone with strangers or people I knew were being shady.

"I was around Puffy, but I kept my distance during the parties. He always seemed shady to me, and he looked at me in a weird way. I saw him look at a couple of young guys like that, and they wound up in one of the private rooms. I don't think they were happy."

Eventually, CDS2 knew it was time to remove himself from the scene.

"It got to be too much. I had to make a decision—do something about what I saw and put myself at risk or get out of the environment. Getting out made the most sense."

CDS2 never told his story to anyone in public until now, for fear of reprisal.

"No one ever threatened me directly. But it was made clear that there would be 'consequences' for not being loyal. But after hearing all the stuff that's coming to light, I got angry. I still don't want to put myself and my family in jeopardy, but I wanted my story to be told."

And apparently, quite a few people want to tell their stories, as the witness list grows right along with the civil lawsuit list.

Chapter Eleven: Sex, Lies & Videotapes

Kim Porter gave us the first glimpse of what a monster Sean John Combs was with the women in his life. While the stories never went viral until his current bag of troubles, any given person who ever worked in the music industry heard the stories of physical and sexual abuse Porter endured at the hands of Diddy.

But he was able to keep his dirty dark secrets in the dark until Casandra "Cassie" Ventura made legal overtures, which created a cascade of legal issues, which finally landed him in prison and in a whirlwind of steadily increasing accusations of sex, lies and videotapes.

But the rumor mill has been running since the early 90's, when he allegedly raped a music producer in New York.

That producer was male.

Rap music was viewed as the most misogynistic and homophobic art form on the scene.

In the late nineties, that homophobia was underscored by the rumors of a gay rapper.

Those rumors were ignited by radio host, Wendy Williams, who started talking about how she had a picture of Bad Boy Records Executive Kirk Burrowes on his knees giving Puffy fellatio.

Williams said that she posted the picture on a website, but in the 1990's, the internet wasn't as vibrant as it would become and there was no social media, so the most traction the picture received was through passing the picture around at industry events.

This was the first crack in the armor of Sean Puffy Combs

In addition, Combs caught hell from the accusations of his relationship with an underaged Usher Raymond, who was living with him while preparing for his entry to the music industry.

Under the current rain of sexual abuse allegations, men are coming forward just as women, with tales of being raped and abused by Sean John Combs.

In his podcast, *Joeversity*, Joe Rogan said that he doesn't believe that Combs is actually gay or even bisexual.

"I'll bet Diddy's not even gay. I think he enjoys fucking guys just so that he can say he fucked them. It's a power move. Also, filming everybody and having dirt on everybody (who participated in the Freak Offs) seems like some kind of organized crime. Like: 'Is this guy doing this on his own?'"

Marion "Suge" Knight, founder of Death Row Records, now serving twenty-eight years in the Richard J. Donovan Correctional Facility in San Diego, California, believes that Combs is simply serving up to others what was served up to him.

In a telephone interview with Michael Franzese, former mob boss, inmate and author, Knight explained that "Everybody knew what was going on with Puffy. The higher ups were doing it to him, and he was doing it to everyone else. That's a cycle that's been going on in the music industry. It was okay to do what he was doing.

"Puffy has been with LA Reid and Babyface. Puffy and Clive Davis were lovers.

"In the gay community, people will say 'they're just gay.'"

The issue isn't that they are gay or bisexual, according to Suge, the issue is they are pretending to be heterosexual.

"These guys are saying they're not gay, they're just having fun."

While there is more acceptance of gay men than there has ever been, there is still a modicum of taboo associated with it, and many people choose to mask it in order to protect their careers.

Suge said that in Hollywood, gay men have to get married right away to protect their reputation.

"When Andre Young (Dr. Dre) told me that he messed with men, I had to get him married right away," Knight told Franzese.

Suge said he believes, just as many others have been repeating, that Combs' difficulties began not with the lawsuit filed by Casandra "Cassie" Ventura, but when he sued Diageo, the company that owns Cirroc.

"He wanted more of the pie. He didn't get what he wanted so he told them he was going to sue them.

"He called them racist. One of the fastest ways to destroy a brand is to call someone a child molester or a racist. They took it as (a sign that) he was trying to destroy them."

Suge said that Diageo, defending themselves, went after Puffy to see what they could find.

"He had skeletons in his closet, and they went to go find them. One thing led to another."

According to Suge, law enforcement knew about him and the kind of people he was affiliated with (drug dealers, for example) because he had been working with law enforcement since he was young and living in the ghetto.

"He was an informant for years. These people act like they're bigger than the law because they are part of the law."

Suge claimed that an officer once told him that the people he was friends with were probably wearing a wire. Suge took that to heart and understood that meant that anyone could be an informant or have a relationship with the police, including Sean John Combs

"They knew his company (Bad Boy) was built with drug money. (Puffy is) somebody who always had a pass and always had favors from law enforcement."

At the Soul Train Music Awards, after Suge secured Tupac's release from prison, Suge recalls that he and Tupac had trouble with the police, while Puffy did not, even though someone with Puffy pulled out a gun.

"I got Tupac out of prison. We were going to the Soul Train Awards. As we were going in, Puffy, Bad Boy and Biggie were coming out, but the police were on us. We saw Puffy go hide in the limo. As we were having an altercation to get past the police, a guy (a gang member from Compton) from a different side of us (pulled a gun).

"Nothing happened to him. Everything goes away."

Suge said that the man with Puffy was in a different gang from Suge's affiliated gang. He also said that the same gang was with Puffy in Las Vegas when he and Tupac were shot, leaving Tupac dead.

Puffy had affiliations on the street, according to Suge, as well as inside of the music industry, including with people who use drugs and sexually abuse children.

"All these people use cocaine. All these people mess with underage boys and girls.

"There's not one person that didn't know that Puffy was fucking Usher (Raymond).

"They had sex with Justin Beiber. That was sad."

Knight told Franzese that no one came after Puffy for what he did to Usher because the focus was on the outcome. Creating a successful artist was the ultimate goal.

"He wouldn't be (the) Usher (we know today). He would be 'the guy that got molested by Puffy' and they didn't want that. They wanted the money."

"It's wierdo stuff because they're involved with pregnant young girls and threatening to beat them up. (Someone) was giving Puffy money from Universal Music Group for hush money."

At the end of the day, Suge said that Puffy is probably a scapegoat for all the people above him who don't want to go down for any of the crimes.

"He might be a weirdo, but a lot of the stuff they're saying he did is true and he's the fall guy right now. Not one celebrity that he hung with is speaking up for him.

"I can't see him falling and nobody else falling with him. I'm sure he's going to tell it all."

Knight explained that Puffy's reputation and freedom aren't the only things that have been affected.

"So many people's lives have been destroyed. It's a bad day for Hip Hop."

Suge said that ultimately, Puffy will be alright in prison.

"They got a lot of baby oil in prison."

Chapter Twelve: Psychology of An Abuser

Sean "Diddy" Combs is facing federal and state sex crime charges, including interstate sex trafficking and sexual abuse of minors. While he tried to cultivate a reputation of businessman, father, friend and even Christian, he has been revealed to be a monster, drugging and raping his victims, some of whom were under the age of consent.

While the general public is talking about Diddy's mentality, his emotional standing and even his childhood, to discuss what kind of person he is and was and what lead him to do the things he has done, few are actually qualified to evaluate him from a clinical perspective.

For this book, I interviewed Dr. April M. Clay, the founder and CEO of Clay Counseling Solutions and the nonprofit, Clay Counseling Foundation. Since 2015, she has led a team providing counseling and behavioral health services to over 2,000 individuals annually in Riverside and San Bernardino counties in California. Dr. Clay holds a License in Marriage and Family Therapy, a Pupil Personnel Services Credential in School Counseling, and a Doctorate in Education focused on Educational Justice. She is a national trainer on restorative justice, suicide prevention, and cultural competence, and has directed school counseling at universities.

According to Dr. Clay, the kind of person who can sink to sexual abuse of men women and children and do so with a system in place, has a tendency to have a clinical diagnosis.

"I'm a therapist and I don't specialize in sex crimes, but generally speaking, looking at basic psychology, the psyche of a person who commits crimes against women and children, there's a tendency for those people to have a diagnosis.

Since Dr. Clay doesn't know Diddy and has not interacted with him in a therapeutic environment, she was understandably hesitant to attempt a diagnosis. She hazarded an educated guess.

"I don't know him, but from what he's been charged with it, it could be said that he's a person with a personality disorder. I'm careful, since I don't really know him.

"We use the Diagnostic and Statistical Manual, 5th Edition (DSM-5) to diagnose individuals. You'll be looking toward personality issues. The more deviant the behavior, the more likely the person is to be associated with something in the psyche that is wrong. You'll be looking at a psychosis or someone who has a personality disorder. Charles Manson, (an infamous murderer and cult leader) is a classic example."

Dr. Clay also emphasized that at the end of the day, she believes Diddy could be treated, based on her dedication to a career of treatment.

"The same way he could be diagnosed, he could be treated. But your treatment is only as good as the person being treated."

Some people, including some of the victims are saying that Diddy's behavior came out of nowhere. Still, others insisted that there had to be signs of his behavior.

"Are there signs? When you say 'out of nowhere' that has to be placed in perspective of a timeline. If they (the abusers) are careful and they can groom you, then you will only see what they want you to see. (For example), If a relative has been in a relationship with a person for thirty years, that's different from knowing a person for three months.

"However, the brain does funny things. We have a sense of familiarity with television and public settings. We tend to let our guard down and subscribe to a sense of safety without having a true sense of safety. They just didn't have an opportunity to know the person first."

Dr. Clay explained that humans tend to romanticize people, especially public figures, based purely on what we see, instead of what we know from gathered knowledge.

"(For example), we see chivalrous behaviors and we place them in a chivalrous perspective, without knowing the anger underneath, or the insecurities that make them go against the activities of chivalry. Then let's add in the role that drugs and alcohol play—that makes a cocktail for behavior that comes out of nowhere.

"With sexual misconduct, you don't see it coming, because it was probably masked because they were sober."

Another piece of Diddy's background that may have come into creating who he has become is the fact that his father, Melvin Earl Combs (who was killed when Diddy was only three years old) was a criminal who may have been associated with notorious New York gangsters.

Diddy has insisted that his father didn't actually work for a criminal enterprise but had his own and was an actual kingpin himself.

Based on the old adage, "the sins of the father will be visited upon the sons," should that behavior have been expected in the child (Diddy)?

"He was three (when his father died), so that goes to the discussion of nature over nurture. Does a person's DNA play a role in who they become as adults? If we open that argument and say that you're born from good seed or bad seed, we will get involved in the person being of (a certain) quality because of their parentage.

"But we know that good people come from bad backgrounds. For example, latchkey kids raised themselves while their parents worked. Maybe the parents were on drugs or incarcerated, but the child becomes a senator. They can always go a different route from their parents.

"If you're looking at Diddy from his genetics, he's made of the same qualities as the rest of us."

According to Dr. Clay, Sean Combs has a history and legacy that is broader than just abuse, so it is important to examine the entire person.

"The man is a whole human and even with the crimes against humans he has committed, he also has a long-lasting legacy of brilliance. You have brilliant celebs who have parents who did nothing notable at all. It's hard to connect those two dots. I could connect the dots to persons who have been exposed to abuse before they began to abuse.

"Theres a connection to a person who is exposed to trauma early in life--especially sexual acts. When children are exposed to sexual abuse, there's a higher tendency for them to become perpetrators themselves."

It isn't know whether Diddy was sexually abused as a child, although allegations point to his own mother. But, a person who abuses others sexually typically has more in the works than simply the pursuit of sexual gratification.

According to Dr. Clay, sexual abuse is associated with power more so than the sex act itself.

"Rape is one of the most primitive acts of violence against humans. The abusers are not getting the adrenalin from the release of the sex, but from the power in the sex crime.

"The act of rape is secret. It's in the dark and no one knows, but they still get a lot out of it. They get off on the control and the power, which is different from the societal power they may have. Both can be in the same person. You can crave the power and the sex (at the same time)."

Chapter Thirteen: Diddy Declining—A Timeline

Before 2023, Sean John "Diddy" Combs was free to roam the countryside, seemingly without a care in the world. He was doing his dirt in the darkness, and it had yet to see the light of day.

However, when you are running an evil empire of sexual crimes, it only takes one person to pull your dark activities into the sunlight.

Casandra "Cassie" Ventura was the first to expose Diddy, stepping out on the world stage with a lawsuit against the monstrous mogul, showing him in all his ingloriousness and vaingloriousness.

Her lawsuit, which was settled in one day, set off a feeding frenzy of legal actions and threats connected to sexual abuse and sex crimes stemming mostly from his infamous Freak Offs.

Here's a timeline to show how Diddy went from mogul to monster in the public eye in less than a year.

November 16, 2023

Cassie Ventura had been in a love and business relationship with Diddy, signing to Combs's label in 2005 and starting a love tryst in 2007, which lasted for just over a decade. During that time, Ventura claims that Diddy raped and beat her "savagely" and controlled her life completely. She also claimed that he would coerce her into sex acts with other men while he would watch during his Freak Offs. Cassie said that Diddy would frequently fly into fits of rage that seemed to be uncontrollable. On 11/16/24, Cassie filed against Combs under New York state's Adult Survivors Act, which establishes a one-year window to file a civil claim, no matter what the actual statute of limitations may be. Ventura also claimed that when she was attempting to flee from him, he eventually caught up to her in

2018 and "forced her into her home and raped her while she repeatedly said 'no' and tried to push him away." And, in the "no one can have you if I can't" department, Ventura alleged that Diddy learned that Kid Cudi, another entertainer was interested in her, and Combs blew up a car belonging to Kudi in 2012.

Nov. 17, 2023:

One day after Ventura filed her lawsuit, Combs made overtures to a settlement for an undisclosed amount, keeping the terms of the settlement private. "I have decided to resolve this matter amicably on terms that I have some level of control," Cassie stated through her attorney Douglas Wigdor. "I want to thank my family, fans and lawyers for their unwavering support." Combs' response was short:

"We have decided to resolve this matter amicably. I wish Cassie and her family all the best. Love."

November 19, 2023

Realizing that other lawsuits were in the making, Diddy began calling another potential victim and even recorded the calls. He asked that victim to support him and give him friendship, while trying to convince her that anything that happened, including potential sexual abuse, had her willing participation. These calls were the beginning of months of calls attempting to to coerce and bribe potential witnesses, according to prosecutors.

November 23, 2023

The day before the expiration of the Adult Survivors Act, two additional women file lawsuits accusing Diddy of sexual abuse. The Adult Survivors Act is a New York law which provides a one-year window for victims of sexual abuse to file civil action, regardless of the statute of limitations.

Filed by Joi Dickerson and an unnamed woman, the lawsuits allege that Diddy committed sexual assault, and that he drugged the victims and beat them.

These acts allegedly occurred in the early 1990's, potentially moving back the start of Diddy's becoming a monster. At that time, Diddy was a talent director and party promoter. Of course, his attorneys called the allegations false.

November 28, 2023

Knowing that more charges are on the way, Combs makes the decision to step down from Revolt, his cable television network.

December 6, 2023

Another lawsuit to add to the pile. This one from a woman who says that Combs raped her and that two other men joined him. The woman alleges that she was flown from Detroit to NYC, where she was drugged and plied with alcohol, which prevented her from consenting to sex with Combs and the other two men.

Combs claps back on Instagram with a strong denial of all the charges and lawsuits. "I did not do any of the awful things being alleged," the post says. "I will fight for my name, my family and for the truth."

February 26, 2024

A man—a music producer, sues Diddy, claiming that he sexually assaulted him. The suit alleges that Diddy forced him to engage in sexual activities with prostitutes. He also provides a detailed list of activities involving drugs and says that he personally witnessed sexual assaults. Comb's attorney claims the allegations are "pure fiction."

March 25, 2024

A strong sign that things are escalating in the Diddy cases come when Homeland Security delivers search warrants during early morning raids on Diddy's homes in LA and Miami. Diddy was in Miami, while two of his children were at the home in LA and were handcuffed while the home was searched.

The next day, Aaron Dyer, an attorney for Combs, labels the raids "a gross use of military-level force." He also says that his client is "innocent and will continue to fight" until his name is clear. Dyer also said that there is "no excuse for the excessive show of force and hostility exhibited by authorities or the way his children and employees were treated."

April 4, 2024

Like Diddy, like son: Another lawsuit—this one in LA-- alleges that Diddy's son Christian "King" Combs sexually assaulted a woman working on a yacht chartered by his father. The suit, which names Diddy as a co-defendant, alleges that he paid for a cover up to protect his son. An attorney claims that the allegations are outrageous.

May 10, 2024

Diddy's lawyers attempt to get a dismissal on the suit that alleged he raped an underaged girl with the assistance of two other men in a NYC recording studio. Their assertion is that the lawsuit missed legal deadlines.

May 17, 2024

The notorious video of Sean John Combs beating and kicking Casandra Ventura in an LA hotel in

2016 is released. It confirms Ventura's assertions in her 2023 lawsuit that Diddy assaulted her as she was attempting to escape his brutality. The world can clearly see Diddy the monster punching and kicking Ventura and tossing an object at her while she is on the floor.

The Los Angeles District Attorney's Office decided that the attack was beyond the statute of limitations and refused to prosecute Combs. The feds, however, cited the beating in their conspiracy case against Combs.

May 19, 2024

In response to the incriminating and embarrassing video, Diddy posts an apology on social media.

"My behavior on that video is inexcusable," he said. "I take full responsibility for my actions in that video. I was disgusted then when I did it. I'm disgusted now. I went and I sought out professional help. I got into going to therapy, going to rehab. I had to ask God for his mercy and grace. I'm so sorry."

June 9, 2024

Howard University, where Combs had studied before entering the music industry, rescinded an honorary degree it had bestowed upon him. It also stopped a scholarship in his name.

June 10, 2024

New York Mayor Eric Adams, responding to the violent beating video, asks Diddy to return the key to the city he had been given in a 2023 ceremony. Diddy returned it and Adams rescinded the honor formally in a letter. Adams expressed that he was "deeply disturbed" by the violent video.

August 26, 2024

Attempting to pushback against the mounting charges, Combs, through his attorneys, asks a federal judge to throw out a lawsuit filed in February by a music producer who alleged that

Diddy sexually assaulted him. Combs' attorneys claim that the lawsuit was filled with "tall tales," "lurid theatrics," "legally meaningless allegations" and "blatant falsehoods" all generated to produce a financial settlement.

September 5, 2024

Diddy plans to turn himself in, responding to an indictment he expects to come down. He checked into a hotel in Manhattan to wait.

September 11, 2024

In a lawsuit stemming from Diddy's show "Making the Band," Dawn Richard, a singer in the group Danity Kane, alleges that she was subject to years of psychological and physical abuse by Diddy. She also alleges that she was groped by the mogul turned monster. Richard, who acknowledges that Diddy helped launch her career, also says in the lawsuit that she witnessed Diddy abusing Cassie Ventura and that she has been living in fear of him.

In response, Diddy's representatives accuse Richard of rewriting history with false claims created to secure a payday and to push her new album.

September 16, 2024

In the lobby of his Manhattan hotel, Diddy is arrested, following a grand jury indictment he anticipated. His attorney claims the arrest is part of unjust prosecution of an "imperfect person" who is "not a criminal."

September 17, 2024

The feds unseal the indictment against Combs, revealing descriptions of him as the leader of a criminal enterprise that pursued sex trafficking, forced labor, interstate transportation for purposes of prostitution, drug offenses, kidnapping, arson, bribery and obstruction of justice. The indictment alleges that Diddy "engaged in a persistent and pervasive pattern of abuse toward women and other individuals," including physical violence, in order "to fulfill his sexual desires, protect his reputation, and conceal his conduct."

Combs appeared before a federal court in New York. He pleaded not guilty to the charges and the judge ordered him held without bail until a trial begins.

ALSO FROM TENACIOUS BOOKS:

DETECTIVE'S AFFAIR

NOTES FROM THE EDGE

IN THE WHIRLWIND OR THE STORM: THE LA RIOTS

THE RAP SHEET MAGAZINE LEGACY COLLECTION

Made in the USA
Coppell, TX
12 January 2026

68223568R00115